THE MARKETING MIX THAT WORKS

A COMPREHENSIVE MARKETING MANUAL TO HELP DENTAL OFFICES GROW

by Jonathan Fashbaugh

Cover art: Alexander Von Ness

This book is based on the author's professional experience in marketing and years of working with dental practices. It is intended to provide general information, strategies, and perspectives to help dentists make more informed decisions about marketing and business growth. Every dental practice is unique, and outcomes will vary. The strategies described here should be adapted to fit your specific circumstances. This book does not guarantee specific results and is not a substitute for professional financial, legal, or business advice. Before making major business or financial decisions, consult with qualified professionals who understand your practice's individual needs.

ISBN: 979-8-9934466-0-8

TABLE OF CONTENTS

INTRODUCTION

THE NUMBER ONE QUESTION that dentists ask me is "How much should I spend on marketing?" Like patients who ask about cost and insurance because it's the only question they know to ask, dentists usually ask about cost and money because it's the only thing they're certain about: "This is going to cost me money, so I need to know how much."

So, I'll just tell you: a successful marketing campaign will probably cost you between $3,000-$6,000 per month.

Now you're probably thinking, "Well, how can you say that? And what do you mean exactly? What's that covering?" et cetera, right? All valid questions, but how about, "How much money is that going to generate for me in return?" I almost never hear that question.

Money spent on marketing should be an investment that provides a return, but because of the radical changes in marketing over the past twenty years and the many unscrupulous marketing companies out there, dentists tend to feel like money spent on marketing is a pure gamble. And marketing companies often have disclaimers that there are no guarantees of anything, so yeah, who can blame them?

Maybe you've tried one or two (or twenty-two) marketing solutions and you're wondering what you're missing. The websites you've had looked decent. Your last website probably looked great when you launched it, but I bet a short while later, another marketing expert told you that it was flawed and the only solution was to start over.

You trust one service after another to get the phone ringing. Sometimes the new patients come in with a little more regularity, but the flood you hoped for never arrives. Before you know it, the steady trickle that got you thinking, "Maybe I found it!" has dried up again, leaving you on the hunt for another marketing provider.

When you ask around about the best marketing company, you get one referral after another of companies you should use, and it seems to be the same list of companies that you've already tried, or you've heard from an equal number of dentists who hate them.

You may have looked to the best and brightest dentist you know, curious about what they are doing for marketing. Their website looks *super* sexy and you know that they are just killing it. Or maybe, their website looks ten times worse than yours—maybe their kid made it for them—and yet, they're drowning in new patients!

Then you try to emulate that recipe for success and instead of a winning formula, you end up right back where you started. You think to yourself, "Ugh, maybe marketing is just a giant waste! Why does it work for other people and not for me?"

You're starting to wonder if anyone really has a clue. You shudder when you think about how much money you've wasted on marketing and you *really* try not to think about the hundreds of thousands of production dollars you've missed out on from patients who went to your competitor down the road.

I've been working with dentists for more than twenty years, and I've run a dental marketing agency for more than a decade. Before that, I worked for an agency that helped doctors in dentistry as well as plastic surgery, ophthalmology, and bariatric surgery. During that time, I've seen what it takes to be successful. I've also seen the pitfalls that can hold a doctor back.

You need a process that nurtures a new patient during their life cycle in your office to truly make any headway. The marketing mix that works, combined with an understanding of the Sales and Marketing Loop I will share with you, will help you build momentum, making both your marketing and sales work better and better over time.

I will share easy-to-use tips, as well as more advanced ideas. Using them, you'll close gaps in your Sales and Marketing Loop so you can consistently generate new patients. This will include how much you should spend on marketing and advertising. The answer of $3,000-$6,000 per month may have blown your hair back but stick with me. I also have another answer—a very different number— that may piss off some advertising professionals. The answer to 'how much should you spend?' may also be *zero* dollars.

Follow the processes laid out in this book and you'll also have a list of next steps. You'll feel more confident about your marketing decisions, knowing which marketing strategies are most likely to get you a return. Use The Marketing Mix That Works, and your investment will be marketing money well spent.

Chapter 1

The Marketing Mix That Works

IF YOU BOUGHT THIS BOOK IN HOPE of finding a recipe for success, you are in luck! It's right here. This is the best dental marketing success strategy:

1. A quality brand
2. Identifies a target patient,
3. Creates a message and,
4. Gets enough marketing and ads in front of that patient.
5. The patient has a need that fits the brand's service.
6. The patient selects the brand by responding to a call to action.
7. The patient receives treatment at the office.

Steps 1, 2, and 3 are critical, foundational components, and we will tackle them, but let's dig into step 4 above. How do you get enough marketing and ads in front of your target patient? What is the tactical marketing mix that just works?

Let's say for the moment that your brand is clean, professional and attractive, and your website is well-built with great content. You've targeted the patient that you want with a message that motivates them. All of that is a complete waste if you can't get it in front of patients.

Your marketing mix should include:

- Search engine optimization (SEO)
- Online listing management
- Online reputation management
- Paid search ads
- Social media marketing
- A data tracking process.

I could write an entire book on each piece of that marketing mix, and if I did, each book would probably be outdated by the time it was published. Even so, I will cover each of these briefly and will tip-toe into some of the areas that may make each of them more or less effective in your office.

SEARCH ENGINE OPTIMIZATION (SEO)

My first job helping dentists with their digital marketing was as a search engine optimization specialist. I applied for the job multiple times and was finally able to transfer within the company that I worked for from the video production arm to its new sister company that offered internet marketing services.

This field was so new that its training was provided as printable pages in a 3-ring binder. It felt like I was learning a newfound, secret science that would magically launch a dental office from online obscurity to the forefront of the web. And back then, circa 2004, that's exactly what it was. It worked. There was a process you followed and websites optimized this way moved up in rankings.

Of course, that secret science didn't stay secret for long and things changed rapidly. The SEO I learned back then only exists in basic principle now. Many of the tactics are now banned by Google. Other optimization tactics have developed since and met the same fate: verboten and to be avoided or you may be blacklisted by Google.

You don't have time to learn SEO much less to keep up with all the changes. Here's what you need to know about SEO as part of The Marketing Mix That Works:

- Your website should be optimized so that Google understands what each individual page is about.

- Google is getting so smart that on-page optimization is much less important than it used to be **but** it still helps, so use it.

- Optimization now extends beyond keywords and incorporates technical components of your website such as load speed. This trend will continue. Rather than get hung up on specifics, always prioritize a website that is easy to use and doesn't inconvenience the prospective patient.

- SEO tactics that work today may not work tomorrow. Work with a company that keeps your website's technology and search engine optimization updated on a regular basis.

SEO is a long-haul strategy that must be used in conjunction with the other components of this marketing mix. It's not a silver bullet and yet, if you ignore it, you'll leave an opening for competing dentists to out-perform you in local visibility.

WARNING: YOUR SEO MIGHT BE GREAT AND STILL MIGHT NOT WORK

Because of all the unknowns and changes surrounding Google, your SEO might be perfect and yet still fail to entice Google to rank your website on the first page for your most desired search phrases. We have a client in a highly competitive market who we have worked with for years on their SEO and they still don't rank on the first page for some of their target keywords. The SEO is done correctly. We've even had third-party consultants evaluate our processes. The only stones we've intentionally left unturned are the ones that Google prohibits as SEO tactics that will get your site banned altogether.

The competition in their market is so fierce, it doesn't make sense to make an investment in additional SEO work. Ranking #1 for 'dentist' is also not one of the dentist's goals. They are a low-volume practice that focuses on a very specific type of patient.

They could try to use ads to compensate for this organic ranking problem but the investment required to stay on top would infringe on their profitability. The website is getting traffic from secondary and tertiary keyword phrases, thereby generating enough new patient leads to satisfy the practice, and their social media exposure is helping them stay in touch with their patient referral base.

I tell my dentists all the time, "I don't have a cousin Joey at Google who I can call and hook my clients up with first page Google rankings." SEO is not reliable as a silver bullet solution to visibility—

especially for fast results. You need it to clarify who you are and what services your practice is known for among your patients.

Pro Tip for Search Engine Optimization: If your web marketing company hasn't talked to you about the quality or quantity of your content, you may want to consider making a change. Many outdated or low-budget SEO companies are happy to sprinkle some keywords here and there in your website and say that their job is done. That doesn't work and it's certainly not worth paying a monthly fee for a company's set-it-and-forget-it work. Good SEO results require ongoing, content-centered work.

ONLINE LISTING MANAGEMENT

Doctors are usually aware that their information should be correct on Google and maybe Yelp, but there are dozens of other websites that list local businesses, and each of these websites matters to a degree.

It's also easy for doctors to assume that, if they correct it on Google, that somehow it will be correct on other websites. This is not the case. Most websites operate independently of each other. There are some important, info-disseminating websites called "aggregators" that feed information to other websites. If the aggregators were all-powerful, we could just focus our work on them, but the websites downstream from the aggregators control what data they pull in and whether or not they use it. Often, they will pull from multiple sources and create new listings that are a mishmash of data to form their own listings.

Google and Facebook also harness the power of their users to crowdsource the chore of keeping their records updated. This is sort of brilliant, but it also opens your office up to incorrect listings.

Keep your information updated across all of these websites. Unfortunately, the job requires ongoing work. You correct one listing and another will go haywire with an old phone number or address or they will drop your web address. It can be maddening but it's worth the effort.

There are a number of tools out there for keeping your data updated. Having tried many of them, I can tell you that none of them are perfect. You will occasionally need your marketing company's help in following up with some websites until your listings are corrected.

Google looks at listing websites to cross reference the data they gather from other sites and the data that you and their users provide them. The more correct the information they find, the fewer problems that you'll tend to have with Google. Google also tends to list websites like Yelp in their listings for many searches, so just because you haven't ever heard of Insider Pages or some other business directory, it doesn't mean that a prospective or current patient will never find the listing.

You can think of these listings as potential holes in a boat. A small, single hole is probably not a big deal, but collectively, too many holes can sink even a giant ship.

Pro Tip for Online Listing Management: Complete your Google Business Profile as much as you can and be sure that you, the doctor, are listed as the owner. This gives your profile the maximum chance at success and makes it unlikely that you'll ever find yourself locked out of your profile and unable to make updates.

ONLINE REPUTATION MANAGEMENT

Would you do me a favor? See, many other doctors have the same marketing problems, but don't know that they can get honest, complete marketing tips like the ones in this book. Would you set this book aside for a moment, hop on Amazon, and write a review about it? This will help me get the word out about the book and will help other dentists like you. I sure appreciate it.

I decided to put that shameless request in this section because reviews are a critical part of the marketing mix that just works. Dentists who are wildly successful have a ton of reviews on Google. More than that, they get new reviews on a regular basis, and most of them are very positive.

Google's ranking algorithm puts a lot of weight on the quality, content, frequency, and number of online reviews that a business has when offering local ranking results. If you're looking for one little tip that's maybe more potent than the others, this is it: try to get at least one new Google review every week, preferably more than one, but do it consistently. Google weights reviews heavily in its ranking algorithms because it's something that they believe will naturally happen when a business is truly great. If it's not so great, it won't be reviewed much and will be more likely to have a negative review. They've also invested in systems that spot and remove phony reviews.

You've probably felt the sting of a negative review or two. The odd negative review is not a big deal. You can even look at them in a positive light as they provide authenticity to your positive reviews. Positive reviews take more effort to cultivate.

You need a system for scanning for new reviews, both positive and negative, so that you and your marketing team can respond to them in a timely manner. Negative reviews without responses will look worse to a prospective patient.

Your marketing company should be willing to help you respond to a negative review. They will have cooler heads than you do and can help you take a negative situation and turn it into a marketing opportunity. When you respond to negative reviews, don't respond to the negative, hurtful, and potentially libelous claims posted by a patient—or an anonymous jerk with too much time on their hands—We know it was you, Karen! No. Instead, take a deep breath and then respond to the prospective patient who is "overhearing" this online conversation and weighing whether or not they want to become your patient. Respond with these components:

- **Truth.** If you're baffled by the review because you have no patient of record with the name, that's okay to call out as long as all of your review responses don't sound start with "We have no patient of record by this name..." But since many profiles on Google and other websites have random, generic names or the name of a business as their profile name, it may not be productive to point out the lack of a name in a purposely anonymous review.

- **Feelings.** If you're feeling hurt, surprised, confused, share that. It's probably not helpful to share that you're angry, but given the right circumstances (ex. abusive language toward the practice or an individual), even that could be appropriate. Sharing your feelings humanizes your practice.

- **Your relevant standard operation procedures and goals.** Share standard procedures and goals to contrast them with the claims in the negative review. If someone says that they had to wait an hour to be seen and that is unheard of in your office, share what should have happened as well as the optimal outcome.

For example: *We're sorry to hear that you had to wait. Our patients almost never have to wait to be seen, and we never want a patient to have to wait in the lobby. Our goal for a new patient exam is to have a patient examined by the doctor and on their way in less than an hour and a half.*

- **What your happiest patients have experienced.** Take control of the narrative of the negative review. HIPAA rules will not let you describe what happened with a specific patient, but you are free to talk about what patients *usually* experience. Talk about those excellent outcomes. If it helps and if appropriate, you can share what can sometimes sabotage patients from achieving success.

  For example: *Our patients rave about the beautiful smiles they have and the long-lasting results that they experience. The only problems that sometimes arise happen when patients don't comply with recommended hygiene schedules or whose lifestyle choices put their restorations at risk.*

- **Invitation for more dialogue.** Even if the situation is case-closed with a particular patient, your response should invite more dialogue to try to resolve the conflict. This is your call to action to the prospective patient and it shows that you are reasonable. Express that you prioritize a fantastic experience at your office and that, when you make a mistake, you do what it takes to make things right.

Pro Tip for Online Reputation Management: Pick up the phone. If you know the patient but have not talked to them yet about their negative experience, the doctor should call the patient. Don't have an assistant do it. If the review was just posted, wait until the following day. Sometimes patients take them down on their own after a day of cooling off. If it's still there, call the patient. Keep a calm, professional tone, but use the same feeling-sharing approach to let them know that you saw the review and were surprised (or shocked, hurt, confused, etc.). Use compassion and ask the patient to tell you why they felt compelled to say the things they did.

Use active listening and share back what you heard them say. If it's not making sense, use the phrase "Help me understand…" and tell them what's not adding up to you—not accusing them of anything— especially not of being irrational. Just tell them what's not computing for you. If there's something you recognize that went wrong and there's a way you can make it right, offer that as a resolution. At the end of the call, ask them if they would please consider taking the review down because you feel that it's not representative of how your office operates, or because it doesn't tell the whole story. Wait another day, and then, if the review is still there, proceed with an online response.

GOOGLE ADS

Before we cover how The Marketing Mix That Works leverages Google Ads, I want to acknowledge a few things:

1. There are many successful dental practices that do not use Google Ads.

2. The best practices for Google Ads will vary among the offices

that use Google Ads because offices differ so much in their focus, location, and competition level.

3. Launching Google Ads is easy but just like with SEO, it's also foolish for a doctor in any sort of a competitive situation to consider managing his or her own ad campaign. Google will *help* you do it. They will do almost all the work for you with their semi-autonomous marketing product. If you go to the Google Ads website, the target audience is not marketing agencies. It's business owners. They make it seem like it's as easy as flipping a switch.

Launching an ad with Google is easy, sure, but turning those ad dollars into patients is much more challenging. Google Ads is built as a universal eyeball delivery system, and they are incentivized to deliver as many people who will click on your ads as they can. They charge you for every click. The algorithm works well if your goal is to achieve the most clicks, but if your goal is to get the right people clicking on your ad, people who will actually show up at your office, it takes massive, ongoing management.

I once received a call from a dental office manager who had hired a marketing company that was headed up by a dentist. The dentist had a practice that was apparently doing well, and had started this marketing company in his spare time. The office manager was excited about the idea of having a dentist run her dental office's ads because this dentist would know which keywords would be good to target. She wouldn't have to teach a marketing company about dentistry.

She was so confident that she provided the marketing company with a substantial budget. At the time, it was the one of the larger budgets that I had encountered for a dentist. There was real money on the line.

The campaign was spending the money without a problem. The people the dentist paid to run the ads were generating a lot of clicks, but the new patient numbers were not panning out. The clicks were not converting into new patient inquiries.

The office manager gave me access to the office's Google Ads account. What I saw was very concerning. The targeting was non-existent. The ads weren't targeting the dentist's immediate area, but instead were available nation-wide, and the campaign included all sorts of keywords that were irrelevant to the dental practice.

The office manager was discouraged. She decided to have Pro Impressions Marketing take over the website, but almost decided to stop promoting it with Google Ads. I was confident that the website was clear and with just a few tweaks would be great at generating inquiries as long as prospective patients could see it.

I was elated when she let us launch a new Google Ads campaign using the same, sizable budget because I knew we could generate a lot of local traffic. The results were fantastic. Lots of great inquires started to come in.

Never wanting to spend more than she had to, the office manager was considering pulling back on the budget because other people that she talked to were surprised at how much her office was spending. She told me later that she didn't reduce the budget because she did the research in her books and found that, during the months when she spent more on Google Ads, they had more new patients the next month. It worked that way almost without fail. She told me this during the same call when she had us increase her Google Ads budget again. They saw even greater new patient numbers as a result.

Most of Google Ads management boils down to a balancing act between thwarting Google's efforts to get absolutely **everyone** to click on your ads (great for Google's bottom line—not so much for yours) and getting actual prospective patients to your website. Trying to get only a specific type of new patient lead is even more complicated.

If you want more dental implant patients coming to your office, you have to understand that, according to Google Trends at the time of this writing, people search for 'dentist' about 15 times more frequently than they search for 'dental implants.' If you decide that all of the people searching for 'dentist,' are looking for a cleaning or they have pain caused by cavities and just need a filling, then you might not want to include 'dentist' as a keyword in your campaign.

Then you have to tell Google that, again and again, in a variety of ways as Google wrestles with confusion, that the 'dental' in 'dental implants,' doesn't mean the same thing as 'dentist.' The robot will continue to try to send you all sorts of related dental searches because to the robot if you want 'dental implants,' then probably 'coconut dental floss' is good too. The Google Ads algorithm will have just as much difficulty understanding why it shouldn't show your ads to someone who types in 'breast implants' on Google.

A good marketing company will understand all of this and will wrestle with Google for you. Your job as the doctor is to help your marketing company know how they are doing. Provide them feedback including:

- Your new patient appointment numbers for the month.

- Your new patient numbers during the same month in the previous three years, noting any significant differences such as office closures.

- Your team's notes on how callers said they heard about the practice.

- Details on the nature of new patient leads (even if they didn't book an appointment).

Your marketing team should be recording calls through call tracking numbers attached to your marketing, but this typically won't include calls directed to your main office phone number. What trends do you see?

- Lots of people asking about a specific service?

- Patterns in wrong number calls or for a specific insurance?

- Comments from patients about having seen an ad or social media post and what they thought?

Err on the side of sharing any concerns or questions that you have rather than holding back for some reason. Through this type of collaboration, your marketing team can refine your Google Ads campaign and save you a *ton* of money. If they don't have this added information, they may believe they are doing a great job when they are actually sending you low-value traffic and leads.

Or you might go on a tear with new patient appointments, meaning that the ads hit on something great, and then it could fizzle. With your input, the ad specialist may be able to duplicate the run of success again and again.

Despite the instant exposure that Google Ads can generate, it is an iterative, growing and evolving campaign. Ads need to be changed up, and the Google Ads platform is constantly changing too. Ad types, policies, and algorithms can all make or break a campaign overnight and require massive changes. Stay in contact with your marketing team and be sure that you're listening to each other.

Great Google Ads management takes time and the goal is to get the cost per conversion down as low as possible. If you give Google $3,000 to work with, and all of the pay-per-click costs total $300 before you generate a new patient phone call (which is a type of conversion), then at most, your $3,000 budget will yield 10 new patient call conversions. But if you can get that cost of conversion down to $100, that same $3,000 budget can then generate 30 conversions instead! That's what proper Google Ads management can do for you.

Pro Tip for Google Ads: Be sure that your team member who answers the phone asks about how they heard about your office and know that an answer like, "Oh, I just found you on the internet," should prompt that team member to dig deeper. You'll find that referrals generate ad clicks, and that's okay. Your ads are still doing their job, making you easy to find. Also be aware that Google Ads will naturally generate a lot of wrong number calls at first. Ask your office's team to log the names of doctors or offices that are mentioned during wrong number calls, then give your marketing team that list. Your Google Ads specialist can try to hide your ads when these names are searched.

Social Media Marketing

The most fundamental social media marketing concept is regularly putting up content, and the nature of the content matters. Decisions about the following nuances really make or break your strategy:

- what to post

- where to post it

- when to post it

- how to post it

- and who to target with the content

Advertising is also an unavoidable part of a successful social media marketing strategy, especially if your goals are to see any sort of volume in views, reactions such as likes, and clicks, comments, or shares (collectively called 'engagement'). You also can't hope to generate any new patient leads without paying the social media platforms you use to get predictable exposure. It's a pay-to-play world. Meta (the name for Mark Zuckerberg's techno-media empire) has stock holders who want to see a healthy bottom line and that won't happen without strong ad revenue.

You should post amazing content but give up the false belief that, just because one doctor did a sexy dance on Snap Chat and was on *Ellen,* your social media campaign has to have that viral potential in order to be successful. That's not really how social media marketing works.

Before worrying about what to post, first decide who your audience is. This lets you then focus on delivering content that is personal, helpful or entertaining in their eyes. Hundreds of dentists are liking and commenting on each other's content, which is fine if that's all they want out of it. But the effort it will take you to become a dental influencer who reaches all those dentists is outsized compared to the return you'll get in new patients. Whereas, an authentically caring, skilled, and successful dental office that also happens to create helpful, entertaining, and personal content while they are conducting the business of dentistry will be more successful at reaching patients, especially with a small ad budget.

Personal content includes the doctor's face. Team members can be a close runner up, so a beloved dental assistant or hygienist is better than canned text and stock images. When the doctor gets in front of the camera though, your content will naturally perform better. This is *social* media, after all, and while dental factoids, and random holiday greetings can add variety to your posts and keep your newsfeed active, those types of posts can't build relationships and trust like the doctor's face can.

Helpful content makes the patient's life better. It boosts your authority and can even be something that patients find so useful or interesting that they feel compelled to share it, which is the penultimate goal for social media marketers. This is especially effective when you tie it to the patient's love of their family and friends. We know that the oral cavity has a huge impact on the total health of the person. When you share a post that says something like, "Bad breath is a warning sign of a heart in danger. Periodontal disease kills. Share with your friends and family for a longer life together," and you include a photo of a heart with a statistic or something like that, you can actually get some traction. It's helpful, touching content.

Entertaining content is usually the most successful type of content on Instagram and Facebook. People who are "doom scrolling" through post after post are looking for their next dopamine hit. Talk about a powerful connection: if you can give a person that happiness hit by making them laugh out loud or at least smile, you're really moving the needle on staying top of mind for them when they or a loved one have a dental need.

Again, for content that really gets results, get the doctor involved somehow. It could be doctor holding up a recent news article about a dental issue. A quick video would be even better. This is why the dancing dentist video was so powerful. The dentist was acting in unexpected ways. He looked like some handsome dude put on a dentist suit and started moving his hips. It turned some heads and made people smile. Just keep the main thing the main thing. As Dr. Constantine, the original "In my Fillings" dancing dentist said on a morning show, "I thought I would get a few laughs and my friends and family back home might see it." Know and play to your audience.

Finally, top it all off with some ad dollars behind the best posts. Your marketing team should be the ones driving this effort. They can boost posts and create ads from your best content that will get even more eyeballs, reaching friends and family of the people who like and follow you. Reaching non-followers will help you grow your follower count and build momentum in your campaign.

Focus your efforts on Facebook and Instagram. Your marketing company should also share most of your social media content on your Google Business Profile as posts. While Google is far from what most people would consider a social media website, the content you share on your Google Business Profile can help boost your rankings.

Do not bother with X.com unless you are a speaker and plan on making money through visibility with dentists. In my experience, dental content does not get patient engagement on X.

TikTok is a great place for video-creating go-getters with family dentistry practices who are looking for volume rather than specific types of fee-for-service treatment cases like implants. If you can build a fun or touching video with a low-cost new patient offer and put some ad dollars there, you'll likely get a response.

You can also build a second career as an influencer on TikTok in a particular niche of dentistry such as Dr. Priya Mistry, The TMJ Doc, but to do so, you'll need to make social media a larger part of your life than you ever have before. If that's your goal, more power to you, but it's not necessary to go to such extremes to be successful with The Marketing Mix That Works.

Pro Tip for Social Media Marketing: Invest in video. Create a space where you can record video and be sure that the office has someone with the latest smart phone as those have decent cameras and microphones. If you have a nice DSLR camera, that's great too, but be sure you're capturing good audio. Whatever you have, use it. All of the social media platforms are hungry for video content, so anything you can make using video will go farther, with photos a close runner up. Text-based images aren't very effective on Instagram. It is a visual platform. If you're struggling with what to record, go to ProViewSocial.com and try the video promp-ting, recording, and editing service provided by my company, Pro Impressions Marketing.

Data Reporting and Analysis

This is the answer to the "Where are the new patients?" question.

If you don't make reporting and analysis a part of your marketing mix, then just keep throwing stuff at the wall. You won't know if it sticks or not but you can just keep chucking money at the problem and hope it goes away. That's what you're doing if you don't prioritize reporting and analysis.

You're the doctor. You don't need to know all the nitty-gritty details, but you do need to have regular meetings with your marketing team. During those meetings, they should share information with you about how your marketing tactics are performing individually and as part of a larger strategy.

The information they share with you should include a summary but also actual data points. Familiarize yourself with them and be sure that they are presented as trends over a period of at least three months. If the period you analyze is too small, you'll make poor decisions.

Do not waste your time looking at weekly data. Even monthly data can be misleading if you aren't tracking trends over a longer timeline. A three-month period will show you one of these possibilities:

- An upward trend where each month is higher than the last.

- A downward trend where the second month is lower and the third month is even worse.

- A fluctuating trend where there are only ups and downs.

All of these patterns then need to be analyzed in the context of the time of year and with year-over-year patterns, ideally with multiple years of data available to you.

If you see a down month or a downward pattern, don't panic. The campaign itself may not be broken. Downward patterns can be caused by external factors:

- Seasonality

- Budget problems (i.e. available funds exhausted or a credit card being declined)

- Platform problems such as ads that were paused by Google or Facebook

- Reporting problems such as a bug in the tracking code preventing data collection

- Market changes such as rising economic concerns

None of these problems are things you want to shrug off without giving them thought, but they are also not indicators that the ads, posts, targeting, or website design are flawed. Of course, data analysis is important because, in the absence of any other plausible explanation, you and your team have to ask why one of the metrics that you track is underperforming.

If traffic to the website is down, you have to talk with your team to find out why. In the case of a decline in website traffic, look for possible issues with:

- Google ranking shifts due to algorithm changes or competition that has moved above your website in the organic (unpaid) results.

- Content that was recently moved, removed or changed on the website, potentially causing a decrease in rankings.

- Content that was added to the website that caused ranking changes. You can gain some rankings while losing other, more important rankings.

- Pages of your site that "fell out of" Google's index, meaning that Google is no longer showing them to its users.

- Ad targeting that was changed, limiting exposure to a smaller group of people, which can be a *good* thing.

If these issues don't give you a potential explanation for the change, then you have to look again at external factors.

When website traffic goes down, your metrics for new patient emails, phone calls, and virtual consults may naturally decline as well. If you see an upward trend in website traffic, you can usually celebrate that there was a good month. If you see an upward trend, even better. But reporting and analysis can help you avoid getting duped.

Have you ever arrived at a vacation destination that just doesn't look like the marketing for the brochure? Those dang fisheye lenses and Photoshop people lied to you! If you don't do a little analysis of your data, a single traffic graph can give you a fall sense of security and excitement.

If your traffic goes up but your leads don't budge or even go down, you still have to go through your checklist of causes. A mismatch in increased traffic without a commensurate increase in leads can mean:

- Your website gained some rankings that aren't relevant for your office.

- The increased traffic is not local to your area.

- Your ad campaign is displaying ads for Google searches or social media users who are not actually interested in the content on your website.

- The new content that brought in more traffic was not "optimized for conversions," meaning that it didn't ask people to take action and contact your practice.

All of the metrics for social media reach, video views, followers, post likes, etc. are great to track too. They are unlikely to have a direct correlation to an explosion in new patient leads. Even ads on social media are more likely to lead to an increase in your social media metrics rather than an immediate increase in phone calls and emails, or even messages to your office. Those come later as lag measures to the work your team is doing on social. This is normal.

What if all of this is tracking in the wrong direction? What if, no matter what you do, the new patients aren't coming to your office? Then it's time for a tactical shift in your marketing.

Without data reporting and subsequent analysis, you would have no idea where your data is trending. If you don't look at the data, you have to take someone else's word as to whether or not things are going as well as can be expected. Data flowing from this marketing mix gives you the ability to make informed, tactical marketing decisions.

ACTION ITEMS

___Look at your Google Business Profile and see if there are reviews that need responses.

___Create a process for monitoring and responding to reviews including practicing for a call to a patient about a negative review that they posted.

___If you are running Google Ads, start creating a list of doctor and practice names that are creating wrong number and other irrelevant calls to your office. Give this list to your marketing company on a monthly basis at first, then quarterly after a few months.

___Create a social media post that features the doctor's face and make it helpful, personal, or entertaining. Feel free to use the periodontal disease post text in this chapter. Bonus points if you can make it a triple threat: an entertaining and helpful post that is also personal because it uses the doctor!

___Find out what reports or dashboards are available from your current marketing company or companies. Ask how often they are updated and set up monthly meetings with them to review the trends.

Chapter 2

Challenges You Know About But Might Not Understand

EFFECTIVE MARKETING AND ADVERTISING is simple when you break it down.

Again, to be successful, every stage of this dental marketing success strategy must be respected.

1. A quality brand

2. Identifies a target patient

3. Creates a salient message

4. Gets enough marketing and ads in front of that patient

5. The target patient has a need that fits the brand's service

6. The patient selects the brand by responding to a call to action

7. The respondent becomes an actual patient who receives treatment at your office.

There's a lot going on there in those seven steps. In step 1, you must understand that a quality brand isn't just your logo or your website. It's what people see when they walk into your office. It's how your employees talk to patients and how they look; how they answer the phone. It's how your office smells and what people think of you after they leave. That whole package is your brand. It must be a quality brand if the promotion of that brand is to be successful.

In step 2, you have to identify your target patient. Do this with intentionality and specificity. This is your chance to "Begin with the end in mind," as Stephen Covey said, and remember the old adage, "Garbage in, garbage out." Push yourself past the easy answers. If you don't, your message may not reach true potential patients, and the information you gather during your data reporting and analysis process won't be very helpful.

Just because you're a dentist doesn't mean your target patient can be anyone with a mouth. Instead, figure out what types of patients make for ideal patients in your office. Be as selective as you can, creating a new scope for your practice. You can offer a number of services, but be sure that they all appeal to your target patient. If there's a disconnect, it will cause problems.

Next, craft a message that appeals to the identity and problems of this target audience, proving that you have the answer to the issues that they face. Rather than spend too much time on this step, I'll recommend that you read Donald Miller's *Building a Story Brand*. It's now in its second edition, and the concept just makes sense. Prove to your target audience that you know what they've been going through and that you have a recipe for success that works. The only mistake you can make is in making the message too complicated and confusing. Keep it short, simple, and honest. After that message is ready, it's time to shout it from the hills during the next few steps.

Steps 4, 5, 6, and 7 aren't necessarily this linear. They become part of a critical loop that you have to keep moving to make sure that The Marketing Mix That Works actually has a chance to work for you. A successful dental marketing strategy can't be a one-time event if you want to see this winning formula come to life in your office. We'll cover each step in detail in this book, including the challenges you may encounter at each stage so you can keep making progress.

STEP 4. GET ENOUGH MARKETING AND ADS IN FRONT OF THAT PATIENT

This is the most common-sense aspect of The Marketing Mix That Works. We know that, if we got a patient from marketing, they will have seen the marketing and responded to it at some point. But I included the word "enough" in the name of this step because The Marketing Mix That Works is not a one-time event or limited-run campaign. It's an ongoing process. This is not a function of what makes the marketing mix successful per se, but derives from the nature of how people work. We have to get their attention at the right time and stay top of mind for them until they have a need and decide to do something about it. This doesn't happen without enough interaction with the patient where they see your brand and know what it stands for.

Search engine optimization and Google Ads try to tap into demand for the services that you offer. As the patient is researching dental care, and then looking for providers, they have to find you, or you will not capture that new patient. The supporting work of online listing management ensures that what people find is accurate, helpful, and engaging information. Online reputation management and social media marketing help to ensure that, when people are looking for more information about you and your office, they will like what they find online and will know intuitively whether or not they will be a good match for your office.

Data reporting will help you track whether or not you have *enough* of all of that happening. You'll be able to track whether people are seeing you online, whether or not they are interacting with your brand by clicking on your ads and listings, and how frequently that is all adding up to inquiries to your practice from people who are interested in becoming patients. This should all work very well and simply, and it does as long as the doctor and the marketing teams are aligned and regularly communicating.

BEWARE A LACK OF STRATEGY AND COMMUNICATION

You can probably sense if your marketing company is asleep at the wheel or clueless about how to market your office. What you might not understand is your role in this situation. If you have no strategy for practice growth, then you will struggle to know whether or not your marketing is achieving its goals.

What are your goals? Why do you want to advertise at all?

If you don't know that, then you won't know who to target with your marketing.

The lack of a defined goal will not stop marketing companies from charging your credit card for their services. They'll just execute the same marketing plan that they have used for other dental offices or even other types of businesses. That may have made other clients happy, but slapping your name on someone else's marketing is more a game of random chance. You need to direct your marketing and advertising campaigns with a strategy, and you need to communicate that strategy with your marketing company.

If building that strategy and figuring out how to communicate it is daunting, start with the broadest strokes and then get more specific. Set literally any goal and then figure out how you'll know whether or not you've achieved it through start-to-finish data reporting and analysis. Want to double the size of your practice? Be even more specific. Use patient numbers or revenue and give yourself a deadline for when you'd like to achieve that number. Be sure to identify how you'll report those numbers as well as leading measurements that contribute to them along the way. These lead measures include new patient leads, new patient appointments, treatment presented, treatment accepted, and collections. Revenue can slip through your fingers at every step of the way.

Maybe you want to own a more lucrative dental practice by netting more revenue per patient. On the business side, that means reducing overhead and streamlining your systems but on the marketing strategy side, it means reaching more people who will say yes to more expensive treatment plans.

What types of services will you focus on to increase your per-patient revenue? You may be a *general* dentist, but don't let that be an excuse to avoid this question. If your direction to your marketing company is "I'm a dentist. I want to do dentistry," then you'll get a mishmash of dental patients rather than patients with a specific need who are seeking a dentist who will provide quality care.

Is this a marketing conversation or a business conversation? Both. Your brand needs to represent itself as the best of its kind in your area—or the cheapest—or the most focused on dental implants—or the dentist to the stars. What do you want your office to be known for? Whatever it is, you have to get specific about the answer to that question and build your dental practice and brand around that idea. This is the way to stand out, and when communicated to your marketing team, it's the only way to ensure they create a marketing message tailored to your practice. It's also a way for everyone involved to measure alignment and progress toward your goals.

STEP 5. THE TARGET PATIENT HAS A NEED THAT FITS THE BRAND'S SERVICE

When a prospective patient or existing patient encounters your marketing, they may not be ready to act on it. On the flipside, when they encounter your marketing, they may realize that they do have a need that they weren't even aware you could address for them. But they will only act on the marketing that they encounter if they have a need *and* see you as the most relevant person to help with their need. Your ad content, social media content, website content, and even SEO should make it clear who you help, the problems that you help with, and how you help solve those problems. If that's not clear, then you are not actually getting proper fulfillment of The Marketing Mix That Works.

If your brand looks like you focus on something else, prospective patients will be confused and will not engage further with your marketing.

AVOID BRAND DISCONNECTS

I once worked with a young dentist who purchased a practice with big loan while still chewing on school bills. The practice was doing very well, focused on cosmetic dentistry. The dentist selling the practice was well-known in the area for giving people Hollywood smiles. My new customer bought a winning practice but was deathly afraid that they couldn't fill the big shoes of the dentist who was selling and moving on.

Despite these fears, my customer and the practice's office manager wanted to build a new type of office that had a spa-like experience, but was still a dental office. We've helped other dental offices who have a spa-like atmosphere, but these guys wanted to do facials and waxing as part of a dental visit or even as a stand-alone service. They hired an aesthetician and asked us to redesign their website that was currently all about dentistry.

We created a mock-up website layout. They didn't like our design. "It makes me want to vomit," the office manager said. This office wanted nothing on their website that felt dental. We took their input and created a new design. The top of the website featured a gorgeous skyline and the other imagery was of flowers, plush sofas, and a bare-shouldered woman with lipstick-caked lips, not even showing her teeth.

The client loved it. "It's bold. It's different. It stands out!" the client said. I showed it to other marketers, feeling uneasy. It was different alright. The other marketers raved about the design too, so we moved on to marketing and advertising.

"We aren't taking insurance. We can't afford to attract people who are all about insurance. We need to attract people who are looking for the best," the office manager said.

I should have asked, "The best...what?" Really, I should have pumped the brakes at the word 'vomit', but in this instance, we failed the client and acted with a 'Yes man' mentality.

The client wanted to keep their pipeline full of cosmetic dental patients while adding aesthetic services. The website still featured dental services, but looked like either a plastic surgery website, a law firm, or a tourism guide website.

I didn't get it and I wasn't alone. We launched the new website and marketing campaign, including paid search ads on Google. The ads got lots of clicks, but people weren't calling or even emailing. Google quickly demoted the website in organic rankings, apparently not understanding the website either. Talking to our search engine team, the urge for them to say 'I told you so' must have been nearly impossible to resist. How can you optimize a dental website for aesthetic services and make it make sense to the average person much less a robot like Google?

The traffic to the website dried up. The new patient leads, which had been coming in steadily before the redesign, dried up. And of course, the client's marketing budget began to dry up too.

The practice was on the verge of closing, but we didn't know it. We had lost the dentist's trust, so we weren't consulted on the solution. The dentist made the call to part ways with the office manager who was driving the aesthetics initiative and hired a consulting firm. The consulting firm had its own marketing team, so we were fired. I didn't argue. The website became a typical dental website.

When I last spoke with the doctor, they said that this marketing change was their last hope. Either this would work and turn things around or the dentist would go back to working for someone else.

To be fair, they had other issues going on than marketing, but the biggest problem they had was brand confusion. People didn't know what this office was. Was it a dentist? A plastic surgeon? A med-spa? They couldn't tell. There was a giant disconnect that led to a giant waste of marketing.

Doctors tend to equate the word 'brand' with a logo. Your logo is the flag that your brand flies, but your brand is the sum of the patient's experience at your office. Marketing and advertising cannot overcome systemic problems in your brand. If the patient entering your office would see, smell, or feel a disconnect with the image of your office that your marketing and advertising presents, you must fix it.

Patients can smell a bait and switch a mile away, and your team will tire of handling the expectations set by your marketing if your dental office isn't set up to handle them. This creates a vicious cycle where the frustrated team fails to deliver the quality and efficiency you need to be successful. No marketing team can overcome this. Marketing cannot change your business. It can only fuel the engine that is already there. And if you put diesel fuel in a gasoline engine, it's not long before the engine sputters to a halt, causing lasting damage.

You must make the changes necessary in your practice to make it conform to the design that warrants top-dollar fees and naturally generates more patient referrals. That type of practice easily generates rave reviews on Google and gets great engagement on social media. It's the type of office that you'll love to own. Your team will love coming to work every day in this type of office too. They'll be almost as proud of your office as you will be.

Or, if renovating your office, hiring new staff members, and training them and yourself to be Ritz-Carlton-level masters of sales and service just isn't something you're willing or able to invest in, then you'll need to contract with insurances and plan on streamlining patient care to do work in volume with a friendly team. Think Chick-fil-A Dental. That type of practice also easily generates rave reviews on Google and gets great engagement on social media. It's just a different lifestyle for the dentist, and the marketing has to be different too, or there will be a disconnect that will impact efficiency.

While marketing and advertising cannot overcome the problems of an office that doesn't provide the best service of its kind in its region, the best-of-its-kind office will get more from its marketing and advertising. The quality of the brand will make every dollar spent on marketing and advertising go further, generating premium return on its investment. Put gasoline in a gasoline engine, and it'll run until it needs to be refueled. Diesel will make a semi-truck tear down the highway for miles and miles. Of course, EVs are going to hum down the road until they need a recharge too. You need a marketing strategy that fuels your practice.

Where should you start? How far should you take this? Look for catalytic opportunities that will have great impact on multiple issues in the practice. Dropping $100K on a new cone beam is probably not wise as a starting point. More on this in Chapter 6, but getting rid of a cranky person answering the phones who hates their job may be a much better choice. If you replace them with a go-getter who is excited to be part of transforming your dental office, you might see more appointments scheduled and fewer conflicts with patients and within the staff.

The pain of making that sort of change will be worth the gain of solving this major brand disconnect. Then you can better tackle changes in your marketing.

DON'T UPDATE YOUR MARKETING WITHOUT A PLAN

You'll be tempted to rush the process of creating a quality brand and to skip the step of creating a message that is clear to everyone who encounters it. Especially after reading this book, you'll want to just toss it at your marketing team and say, "Build me a new logo and website. This one is old and sucks!"

Don't give in to that urge. Take the time to get it right by making a clear plan. Yes, your logo should look great, but unless you take the time to write down who you want to attract and what you want to say to them, you won't be able to communicate that plan to your marketing team.

If you're a whiteboard person like me, go crazy with a web of circles, arrows, and crossed-out ideas until you're left with a vision of your ideal target patient and what you want to say to them. Distill it further. Write it out. Verbalize it with your family, friends, and team until you can address every question it elicits and you've eliminated all ambiguity. You'll be left with a clear brand message.

As you go through this process, building a distinct, focused dental brand message, you'll grow painfully aware that your old marketing—perhaps even your logo—no longer represents your brand, nor is it suited to achieve the goals of your marketing program. Those should be the reasons to update your marketing. You'll realize that your marketing isn't just old—it's irrelevant. It will feel like someone else's marketing.

Your new brand message will guide the evolution and upkeep of your marketing. Be picky and discriminating about what is added to your marketing mix. Be bold in turning down what other dentists, who have no strategy or distinctive brand, are just tacking onto their marketing "*plan*." Unless it fits with your strategy and is complementary to your message, it has no place in your practice's marketing.

Also be bold in adapting and investing in keeping your marketing updated. It's a balancing act. Keeping your website, ads, content, social media, and other marketing tactics fresh can have many benefits that generate more new patient leads. Don't be so enamored with your new marketing that you never change things up. If you do, you'll wake up one day realizing that what was so "you" at one time is irrelevant now.

STEP 6. THE PATIENT SELECTS THE BRAND BY RESPONDING TO A CALL TO ACTION

You have to ask for the sale in your office. Imagine if, during an exam, you explained how a procedure works and then just walked away. Eventually the patient would just get up and say, "okay then, I guess

I'll be going…" They'd feel really awkward. That awkwardness can exist online too. The marketing mix that works can help you get your message out to the internet, but the message needs to include a clear call to action that shows the way.

This problem is most visible on websites. If all of your buttons say Learn More, your phone number is hidden at the very top or even the very bottom of your website, and the Contact button in your website navigation is the only part of your website that seems to allow interaction, you are missing out on new patient opportunities.

This has even become a tenant of search engine optimization. Google knows how people use your website, and if prospective patients seem to meander about a bit and then leave your site without having converted, Google will assume that your website didn't do a very good job. The algorithm will make note that maybe your site shouldn't be so highly ranked. It's one of many signals Google uses, but user experience is a verified part of Google's algorithm for organic listings and Google Ads ranking as well.

If you want to increase the efficiency of your marketing, make sure that your target patients hear your message *and* hear you ask them to contact your office for an appointment. If you don't think that's happening as often at your office as at other dentists, look around at what your competitors are doing and you may see some clues.

Don't Be Blind to Competition

You should know that your first and greatest challenge is competition. One of my mentors, Bill Fukui, always said, "Great marketing is not formed in a vacuum." I can see him standing at his desk, headset to his ear with a potential client on the phone, hands gesturing in the air.

He said this to doctors again and again, trying wrap their minds around the idea that dentists can't afford to create their marketing as an act of navel-gazing. You have to be aware of what your competitors are doing.

The goal of competitive research isn't to find out what the other guys are doing just so you can copy it, but so you can see how your marketing will appear to patients who see you and see your competitors. Is there an obvious choice when you put your marketing up against the guys and gals down the street? There should be. If the competitors are the obvious choice, you must adapt!

Remember that a brand disconnect may be at the source of your challenges. If your competition doesn't have this brand disconnect, that alone might be the source of the je ne sais quoi that makes them the better choice over your sexy new website. Does their team love their office and what they do? Be bold and ask yourself the hard questions about what makes the competition your actual competitor. Then be humble enough to list the changes you must make.

To be clear, as I said in the previous section, you don't want to copy everything that your competitors are doing, especially when doing so would not be synergistic with your brand and message. When you've got an awesome office, you'll find that many other dental offices in your area hardly qualify as competition because they pose little threat to you. They serve a different patient than the ones you are targeting. So why copy what those practices are doing?

ACTION ITEMS

___Write out the marketing goals you want to achieve in clear, quantitative terms.

___Describe your ideal, quality brand using feeling and experience-oriented language.

___List the changes in your practice that you must make in order to make your practice align with your ideal, quality brand. Set realistic deadlines for when you will make each of these changes, writing them down next to each change you must make. Reorder the list as appropriate.

___Review your marketing tactics and results, not making changes yet, but just to make sure you are familiar with the state of things. Include the number of new patient appointments and new patients seen on a monthly basis for the last 24 months.

Chapter 3

Hidden Challenges

IN DENTAL MARKETING, it sometimes feels like you're doing everything right—you are matching your competitors blow for blow in marketing tactics and even quality—and yet they are still eating your lunch. It's crazy. It's unfair. Why is it happening? There are some hidden challenges that you might be facing. It could be some of these or all of these. You have to dig deeper before you have any hope of turning your results around.

Even if you're using The Marketing Mix That Works, if you wrestle with these issues, you'll be sabotaging your effort every step of the way. No amount of SEO or ads or even social media marketing is likely to make a difference until you uncover these hidden challenges.

Marketing ADHD

We all feel the pressure to grow our businesses. You *need* new patients to grow your practice. Your marketing company should understand and share that pressure. There is a temptation to chase after the latest thing that hits your radar regarding marketing. This can be a mistake—not always, but it can be dangerous to be twitchy with your marketing.

I once had a customer who was in a tough market and had a bad reputation in his area. We were doing everything we could to overcome these challenges. We got him on the first page of Google in his area for most of his priority keywords in both the natural rankings and paid ad results. We were making the phone ring and I was pretty happy with our lead numbers. They were comparable to other offices in much more favorable circumstances.

Then one day, I got a call from him. He said, "Jonathan, I like you. I like what you're doing for me, but there's this other company who charges a lot less and they've got a plan to get me more leads. I already gave them the go-ahead but if things don't work out, I'll be back."

I was shocked and very suspicious on the client's behalf. The new company took over and blew up his website (and not in a good way). They changed everything; made several very well-known marketing mistakes. We still had access to his data and I saw his results going down the tubes. I contacted him to let him know what I saw but he decided to let the company continue for a few months. Unfortunately, during that time, the damage had really taken its toll.

The client returned but at that point, our job was really to pick up the pieces. We reverted the website, but Google no longer trusted it as a stable website and its rankings were a struggle. We slowly regained speed and after a year, had just about gotten things back to where they were…

Then my phone rang.

It was the good-for-nothing client! I'm just kidding. He's a sweet heart of a guy and I love him. But he was jumping ship *again*! The entire story repeated itself: the website was torn apart; the rankings tanked. Everything happened again. This time, I didn't contact the client. He reached out to me. "Jonathan, never again. This is horrible. The phones are dead. Will you take me back? I'll never leave again." It felt like a bad, on-again-off-again relationship. I said 'Yes.'

I shouldn't have. Almost a year to the day, the client decided to leave again! To this new company's credit, they didn't tear things apart, but the dentist's marketing ADHD caused a giant waste of marketing dollars.

It's a mistake to make twitch decision after twitch decision, giving into the marketing ADHD temptation that says, "Maybe this thing is a little better. I have to try."

When you make tweak after tweak, twitch decision after twitch decision, you doom your marketing to failure. The hidden challenge here is to be at peace with the long game and to continue building momentum. Being first to try out a new marketing tactic is usually a bad move. Why should you be the guinea pig? And being a lemming to jump over to a hot new company just because some of your colleagues are using them…? You have to seriously examine the upside and whether or not your goals will be better achieved with any change.

Use the scientific method to boost your odds of winning. Collect data over at least three months before you make a change to any sort of marketing and even after collecting that data, try to measure it against another time period that is as comparable as possible. Any experiment with too many variables will produce specious data at best, and will require further testing.

Stay the course and introduce new strategies carefully, one at a time. Remember that stopping a strategy is actually introducing a new variable too.

Pro Tip for SEO: A new website will almost always take time to come to the surface in Google results, even if it's well-optimized. Marketing companies should set this expectation, and they should warn you that, if you completely revamp a website, it can throw Google for a loop and temporarily set you back. It doesn't always happen, but it can. If you launch a new website and it has been a few months, and you're still not where you want to be on Google, you still have to give it more time. If you feel your patience waning, leverage ads to get you the exposure you're lacking on Google, but don't give into fear. Pulling the rip cord prematurely will force you to start all over again. SEO requires patience.

VICINITY

For a long time, Google has worked on finding relevant local results for its users. "Near me" searches on Google peaked in 2021 and have been trending down steadily ever since, likely to become a thing in the past as Google, Apple, and other platforms learn everything about us starting with our locations, then tailor their results to our needs. For dentists, the old adage, "Location. Location. Location," matters when it comes to the internet as well as in the real world.

The hottest hot spots in your town are hot because they are great *and* because they're usually not too far off the beaten path. Convenience matters. A good location does more than make it easy for people to get to your location when they need you. A good location also doubles as advertising. People drive by and see you regularly—daily—maybe even multiple times per day if you plan it right.

WHERE ARE YOU LOCATED ONLINE?

If people have to wander too far down the page of Google's search results, and I'm not even referring to page 2, but just going down too far on page 1 of Google's search engine results, you're not going to be a 'hot spot' on the internet.

My friend once invited me to this cool little coffee shop to meet and talk about business. The coffee was great, as was the decor and service. I could have seen myself breaking out my laptop and working there at times, but I haven't been back since that day. I remember when I used my GPS to find the place, I put in the name of the coffee shop. I didn't search for coffee shops in my area. I only went to it because my friend told me. That's great for that business that my friend was willing to recommend it, but since it was tucked away in a side street of my little town, I'm probably not going to be back any time soon. I just don't take that street much.

Your dental practice can't afford to just show up when people search for your name. Nor can you subsist on the odd patient who happens to find you one time when they search for a peculiar dental-related phrase like, "dentist who fixes teeth and makes your breath smell good." You need to show up for both of those things. Your name is your brand. Niche services are what may just make that patient a raving fan about you. But you need to have consistent visibility for the main-street-equivalent phrases for your most important services. If you're a general dentist, this means 'dentist near me.' If you're a cosmetic dentist, that means 'cosmetic dentistry.' And yes, dominate the side streets like 'porcelain veneers' and 'TMJ treatment.'

Your office website needs to show up everywhere it can. In that way, it has something that your physical office never could—not unless you belong to a corporate chain of dental offices with a location at every major intersection. That's where the eyeballs are. That's where you get drive-by visibility.

Here's the hidden challenge: Google gives dental offices in the vicinity of the user high priority in search engine placement. If your practice is located on the outskirts of town, and the vast majority of your target patients are in the epicenter of the city or across town, you're almost certainly out of luck when it comes to organic listings in the maps area of Google's results.

If you are about to move your office or start up a practice, I highly recommend Googling the name of your city, clicking on the map, and looking at where Google drops the pin in the map, identifying that place as what Google considers the epicenter of the city. The farther away your new location is from that pin, the harder it will be for you to rank for 'dentist City Name.'

A good second rule of thumb for larger metros is to try to stay inside your city's major ring road highways. If you are outside these ring roads, and especially if your actual physical address is not the name of the big city, but is instead the name of one of its suburbs, you'll be much less likely to show up in Google search results for anyone who is in the city proper. You'll have to pay more for ads if you want people to drive out to you, and having a niche will be even more important unless you're content with the population of your suburb and those of areas further outside of town.

In December 2021, Google doubled down on this. They changed their algorithm, making it even harder for businesses located on the outskirts of town to achieve organic rankings in major cities.

If that's you, to target the heart of your metro area: make the painful—seemingly impossible—physical move of your office to a more "convenient" location where you'll be more attractive to Google and more passersby. Or get out your wallet and pound the area with ad dollars. Your cost per patient will go up, but if you're worth the drive and can differentiate yourself from your competitors, you should be able to make it work.

Pro Tip for Online Listing Management: Max-out and manage your Google Business listings. Google really does treat Google Business Profiles as the social media platform that businesses should focus on. If you're struggling for visibility due to a vicinity issue, in addition to Google Ads, be almost hyperactive on your Google Business Profile. Add new photos and video to your listing on a monthly, if not weekly basis. Run contests with your existing patients on who can post the best photos of themselves, you, and your office. More photos posted by active Google users (who are not you) are strong, positive signals that people go to your office and enjoy their experience.

In general, when Google presents you an opportunity to leverage your office's message, you want to do it, so max out those opportunities and stay on top of regularly doing so as new opportunities arise on a somewhat regular basis.

YOUR REPUTATION PRECEDES YOU

Imagine your worst patient. Pull their face to mind and remember the situation and how it went bad. Think about how uncomfortable it would be to share an elevator ride with them or sit next to them on an airplane. Now ask yourself how many of their friends and family are likely to become patients in your practice. Probably zero and it's because of that tension and animosity.

Do you know how much of that animosity can be found on the internet? Unless you have ongoing online reputation management happening as part of The Marketing Mix That Works, you probably don't. You don't know what you don't know and if you have a knot in your stomach right now, maybe you don't even *want* to know how much negativity is out there surrounding your name or your practice's brand.

I'd love to tell you that it's okay, but it really isn't. Google rarely shows organic results for providers with terrible reputations. They have to really be at a loss for results to show someone that they believe their users just don't like or... might not like.

They work to predict the user experience and if you have negative reviews or less visible negative content such as multiple malpractice lawsuits in your past or present, Google will find them and they will hold this against you. Maybe you had your license suspended from a past event. There's a record out there somewhere. While people may have to dig to find those things, Google's legion-minded algorithm has all the time in the world to cross-reference Justia, Ripoff Report, or even relatively small, unknown websites.

If you have a few rough spots in your past, most likely the best you can do is to counter balance the bad with shining 5-star reviews. Start by ensuring that you have a dental practice that people would naturally want to rave about, and then ask for those reviews. This will help Google understand that those disagreements, misunderstandings, and mishaps are all in the past.

Pro Tip for Online Reputation Management: If you can't beat a bad listing, bury it. It really is all you can do sometimes. Double-down on efforts to achieve new 5-star reviews, but also look for new opportunities to achieve branded search listings: things that will show up when someone does an online search for the doctor's name or practice name—whichever one is currently being dragged through the mud. You may not be able to ditch that smudge on your reputation, but you can probably make it harder to find and create positive listings that will shine brighter than this dark mark.

WHAT GOOGLE THINKS ABOUT DENTISTS

It's likely that Google believes prospective patients need websites (and dental practices) that meet these criteria:

- Is the website fast and easy to use?

- Where is this dentist located?

- Does this dentist see patients like the user?

- Can they help solve the user's problem?

- **Can the user go to this dentist with their current insurance (or afford it without insurance)?**

- Will the user like this dentist?

- Can the user trust this dentist? What do other people think?

- How can the user contact the office?

- **Can the user take their kids there too?**

There are two troublemakers there. If Google believes that all its users either have insurance and want to use it (meaning an in-network benefit), then fee-for-service offices may struggle to rank for general dentistry terms. Many dental offices begrudgingly see kids or will accept patients in their teens, but don't proudly market themselves as family dental offices. These may be the real reasons why Google seems to love DSOs.

If these patient priorities are believed by Google, then Google's algorithms may naturally reward dental offices that:

- Are geographically closest to the user. (Google has confirmed this.)

- Seem to be relevant to users who click on their websites.

- Seem to offer the services users are most interested in.

- Accept insurance and are in-network with various plans.

- Will be able to serve the entire family.

- Are easy to contact.

Because everyone has general dentistry needs, it makes sense that

Google would assume they need to find a general dentist who specializes in being a general dentist rather than a practice that flaunts being unique, focused on cosmetic dentistry or another service, and is a fee-for-service practice.

Many dentists have been fighting the good fight for decades, trying to educate the world that the insurance companies should not dictate the quality of care that people receive and that their mouths are worth investing in for improved quality of life. It's a worthy cause, but you have to know that, if you're adamant about being a fee-for-service practice, you'll have to market your practice differently, and have a worldclass team who knows how to sell and deliver value.

COLLEAGUES LIE

Is this all too difficult to hear? Do you find yourself looking for the 'easy' button? Your colleagues on social networks and dentist forums will occasionally tell you that, "Eureka!" they've found it! You just sign up with Company X or start using Product Y and bingo, you win the internet lottery for new patients.

How many times have you listened to that colleague's advice and for some reason, your results are not what they described? The reason is simple: your colleagues lie. Sorry, but it's true. They don't mean to mislead you and they usually have no agenda but to try to be helpful.

The problem is that they are not marketing experts. The story usually goes something like this:

Doctor Smith signs up for a new service that he was sold on. The service reports some early success. Sometimes the success is just that the service helped his ad reach a bunch of people. These people didn't even contact the practice, but the report look impressive. Doctor Smith shares this apparent success but instead of describing it accurately as ad impressions (people seeing his ads), he says that he's getting patients from it.

Or, perhaps he is told that he is getting a lot of new patient leads, and that's what he tells the group on Facebook or in an email forum. The problem is he doesn't know that more than half of the leads are bogus or from people looking for free dentistry. They might even just be people requesting a free price quote and all he has is their email address.

The final scenario is that Doctor Smith is already #1 on Google for all of his keyword phrases because he has been investing a ton in branding for decades. He signed up with Product Y on his website and that new widget is dinging like crazy. The way he describes it, it sounds like Product Y made his website an overnight success but when you add it to your website which is on page 8 of Google, your Product Y feels like Product Why Did I Bother? It doesn't do anything because you don't have Doctor Smith's visibility or brand recognition. You also don't know that Doctor Smith's call volume went down because the widget took attention away from other calls to action.

Your colleagues may know more about marketing than you do, but that doesn't make them marketing experts. They may just be parroting sales language that they heard and are regurgitating incomplete or erroneous data. This can cost you a bunch of money and momentum if you deviate from your marketing plan to try to copy someone else's success with the latest fad.

Instead, you need to tailor your marketing around your practice—your market, your goals, your office, your team—all of this is not identical to your colleagues. Use The Marketing Mix That Works, detailed in the next chapter, and tailor it to your office rather than using a marketing tactic that is reported to work at someone else's office.

Pro Tip for SEO: Colleagues unintentionally lie about SEO a lot. There are some tricks out there that SEO companies occasionally stumble upon. Often, they don't even know why something works, but they exploit it for as long as they can and love to tell their customers about a big win. The trouble is, these tricks never last. A doctor can sometimes be told about this amazing result by their SEO company's rep. The doctor gets excited, sometimes even getting into the nitty-gritty, super-nerdy details about what the SEO company is doing. Then, thinking that they've found this secret SEO sauce, they'll start telling colleagues, "Hey, you've got to go try XYZ SEO. They are doing some really innovative stuff that's getting great results." It's sort of true, but not, because the SEO company just got lucky and was able to benefit from a glitch.

By the time other dentists decide to switch to XYZ because of Marketing ADHD, the glitch has been fixed by Google. The trick doesn't work for these dentists who tried to hop on the bandwagon, and often, their results end up worse off than what they were doing before. Not often, but sometimes, the dentists end up really getting hosed because the trick is against Google's terms and conditions, and can end up getting a nastygram from Google saying that they've been removed from Google's results due to a violation of their terms of service. It's a long road coming back from that.

Action Items

___Identify when you last changed your marketing company and when you changed it the time before that so you can come to terms with whether or not you've been suffering from marketing ADHD. If you're feeling tempted to make another change in marketing companies, outline the reasons why and what you've done to try to work through your concerns with your current marketing team before you make another switch. Consider "switching" to your current company by rebooting your campaign from the start using a clearly communicated strategy and goals.

___If you live in a metropolitan area, Google the name of the major city nearest you and click on maps. Identify what Google considers your city's epicenter and how far away you are from that epicenter. If the drive time to that location is greater than 15 minutes, note that you'll likely need to use Google Ads to pull leads from that side of your metro area.

___Outline how your practice may differ from what Google considers the ideal dentist and compare any disparities against your goals for rankings. Adjust your expectations, goals, and strategies accordingly.

CHAPTER 4

TACTICAL DECISION-MAKING

I DON'T THINK ANY BUSINESS owner would purposely opt for a set-it-and-forget-it marketing strategy. You don't want to have to be the one constantly prodding your marketing along, nor do you want your marketing company to launch the site and let the marketing campaign coast from there. You might opt for a one-time marketing initiative intended as a shot in the arm for your practice, but if you're paying money every month for marketing, you would never be satisfied with marketing that was done once and then left unattended. Unfortunately, that's what a lot of marketing companies end up providing. They offer reports but don't have the drive or ability to launch and to continue working The Marketing Mix That Works, especially when it comes to really tracking the data.

I worked at an agency that had more than 400 clients. Some were dentists, others were plastic surgeons, ophthalmologists, bariatric surgeons, and a hefty helping of lawyers. I held various positions in the company during my six years there and the company grew rapidly during that time. The team tried to track results and adapt but there was just too much coming too fast. Despite the smart team and savvy leadership, things constantly fell through the cracks.

By the time I left the company to start my own marketing agency, I was the senior sales consultant. I realized I was signing up clients who I knew would be desperately unhappy in six months, and canceling a year later. It was disheartening. I knew that if I were managing things on my own, I could do better.

I launched my own company in 2010. The first three years of working for myself were crazy. I learned a lot and the internet changed radically again and again. In 2013, I brought on a partner and formed a new marketing business. All of our customers were dentists so we made it official: we were a dental marketing company. We called it Pro Impressions Marketing Group.

The company grew slowly and that has been the secret to our success. I enjoy making a good living and if I had thrown a can of kerosene on the thing to spike growth, I might have made even more money for a short time, but the company would have flamed out. Instead, we focused on quality of service and retention.

We've lost very few clients since the company's inception in 2010 and many of the ones that got away over the years have come back. I'm sharing the story of my business because I think you should be able to see some parallels.

Pro Impressions Marketing succeeds because of three things:

1. Our dentist-only niche.

2. Effective communication, making client service our top priority.

3. Sound tactical decision-making with the goal of being more profitable every year.

Doctors are forced to make quick, often underinformed decisions about their marketing. Sometimes, they decide not to make any decisions and just leave things in cruise control. If the new patients are flowing, I can't fault them for that. Don't mess with a good thing, right?

The trouble is that you may take a look at your current state of affairs and believe that you've got a dumpster fire on your hands when often a good thing is happening but it's still in formation. What if God saw the first cocoon from his first caterpillar and said, "Well this thing sucks!" and winked it out of existence? We would never have had butterflies.

Tactical decision-making should be incremental over time rather than radical, instant, and rash. Doctors get this wrong more often than not until they learn that marketing takes investment, patience, time, and a scientific approach.

The marketing mix that works includes data tracking and reporting because dental marketing success requires data-driven decision-making and curiosity. Many doctors use decision-making that reveals that they think of marketing as a total gamble or purely transactional. They act like they are placing bets at a horse track or hiring a plumber to fix a sink.

To these doctors, their digital marketing campaign *is* their website. And you build a new website every year or so, right? *Why not give these guys a try. Meh, that wasn't great. Let's try this web designer I met at church this year.* Or *I'll let my kid have a crack at it.* The problem is that, in these scenarios, there is no real planning happening, and no analysis after-the-fact to see how the decision impacted the practice. If you don't look at your marketing as part of your businesses, it can never truly contribute to your success.

You *do* have to make changes. The set-it-and-forget-it approach is just as dangerous as getting twitchy with your marketing dollars. The balance lies in curiosity and patience.

Find a marketing company that you think you can trust and work with them as long as they can show you progress during your meetings to go over your campaign reporting.

Be curious about what they are doing. Your marketing rep should be able to tell you what they did and how it worked. If the last change they made was a stinker, don't immediately kick them to the curb. Be curious. If they say that the new ad campaign didn't generate the new patient flow that they thought it would, ask, "Why do you think that is?"

If they don't have an answer as to what they think may have happened, or if you get a whiff of a lie in how they present things to you, it's time to find a new provider. They won't always know exactly what happened. As marketers, we never have all the data, but we have enough to form theories and to form a new hypothesis to test.

You might think, "I don't want to hire people to test things with my money. I want to hire people who **know**!" This is important: the only thing that marketers know are outcomes of what they did yesterday.

Remember what I tell my dentists? "I don't have a cousin Joey who I can call." Google is under constant scrutiny to keep things fair and they've built a system that makes money when businesses have to keep paying to get results using ads. Whether it's organic SEO or paid search, Google is a fickle frenemy.

The marketing environment is always changing. Google's algorithm changes are classic curveballs that online marketers have to try to connect with. Streaming threw traditional media experts for a loop. Now I'm wondering how long the modern website will live before it gets swallowed by the virtual reality metaverse, or by generative AI interfaces like ChatGPT. Things always change, but if your response to these changes is to restart your campaign again and again, you will lose. Instead, get curious.

Collaborate with your marketing team to explore your options and make some predictions. Set monthly meetings to analyze the data and follow the progress of the current plan for at least three months at a time.

It takes work; time and money. Your marketing company should take this seriously. Your marketing dollars represent a significant investment and a massive gesture of trust. You could spend those dollars on a number of different things, including a marketing campaign run by a competing agency. They should get that without being told. If you don't get the feeling that this is the case, let them know that they are on notice for that reason alone.

In the previous chapter, I shared some critical tips on data tracking and analysis. Those are critical and your tactical decision-making should be triggered based on your findings during that tracking and analysis process. Your decisions will form the third part of a three-part, circular process:

1. Track the data. Record what's happening.

2. Analyze the data. Know what happened.

3. Tactical decision-making. Decide what to do now.

After step 3, you go back to step 1.

All of this supposes that your tactics flow from a sound strategy. Do not ignore these elements:

1. Who am I targeting as my homerun patients, and who am I willing to accept as base hit patients? A base hit can win the ball game in the long run.

2. Why would these people choose me for their treatment instead of my competitors?

3. How will I turn the leads into revenue?

Your tactical decision-making should always touch back to these three questions. If you and your team—that is, your team at the office *and* your marketing team—are not clear on those three points, you will have dysfunction in your marketing and sales process.

Let's start with #1.

WHO AM I TARGETING?

You don't want your marketing team patting themselves on the back for something that they perceive as a win when you don't even see those wins as base hits. I always tell new hires at our company about teeth whitening in this light. Consumers equate cosmetic dentistry with teeth whitening, so I have to re-educate a new team member that our average office is not very interested in spending money to generate teeth whitening patients. They want patients who are interested in more extensive treatment. They don't mind people asking about teeth whitening, but it's not something that warrants aggressive pursuit.

If your marketing company doesn't understand what your loss-leaders are and what a true win is, close that communication gap. Get collective clarity on who you want to target. Then the team can tell you how they believe they can target those people.

If your data analysis shows that the leads you receive are not homeruns or base-hit patients, or if the leads are totally MIA, you have to look at your targeting. Get curious.

- Is there a disconnect between your ads and the content that you are promoting?

- In search ads and organic search marketing, does the search team understand the most desirable keywords your target patient is likely to use when looking for an office like yours?

- Is your content (i.e. the video, web page, social media posts) relevant and focused on the needs of your target patients?

- Is there a mismatch between what you want to target and your immediate market that would mean a lack of available patients?

- Is there a disconnect in the placement of your ads and your target patient demographics?

The data should be able to show you how your campaign is

performing. Your marketing team should be able to fill in most of the rest of the answers to these questions. Some of it will also be common sense once you ask the question but can be tricky to identify as problems if you don't look at the problem from all of these angles.

A dentist I know, Dr. Rod Strickland, used this scenario when teaching marketing. You develop an amazing commercial that promotes high end dentures and dental implants. You even hired a video team to record patient testimonials in your office. It's the best commercial for dentistry that you've ever seen. Then, what if you got a great deal on some television air time? That'd be a win to keep your cost per phone call or website visitor down. You green light the spot and wait for the phone to ring and all you get is crickets.

The problem? That cheap airtime was during the middle of the night on a channel geared toward young people. Or, in the streaming age, it'd be like displaying your video ads in front of VanossGaming content. Don't know what that is? Neither do seniors who want dentures and implants! It's a loser of an ad placement.

You want your advertising to get in front of your ideal patients.

Pro Tip for Online Advertising: Demographic targeting and retargeting aren't silver bullets. I've heard dentists I respect—docs who teach dentists how to be successful in business—refer to retargeting and demographic targeting as advertising must-haves. I would bet money that they're just repeating things that marketing gurus have said without really looking at whether or not true retargeting is being leveraged for their offices. It's another case of "colleagues lie."

Demographic data is hard to come by. When you leverage

demographic targeting in Google, it almost always shows that it has very little to go on. This can lead to embarrassingly-low numbers of impressions as Google tries to target the people who you may identify as your ideal patient due to income levels or gender. The data just isn't there for most users due to health information privacy laws.

HIPAA has also hindered medical businesses from leveraging retargeting. Reputable marketing companies who learn that the customer is a medical or dental provider will usually decline to use retargeting because they want to avoid liability for themselves and for you, the customer.

Retargeting requires code to be placed on the website that can, to the trained eye, reveal that you are snooping on the user's computer, collecting data that can contain protected health information. Advertising networks leverage this data to serve the user ads that follow them around the internet, reminding them about your brand. There are work-arounds and people who say that they've gotten around this issue successfully, but the general consensus is that when you cross this data-collecting line on the user level, you're asking for trouble. And if you don't cross that line, then you don't actually have the info you need in order to make a retargeting campaign more targeted than a standard display advertising or search marketing campaign.

Steer clear of retargeting until you hear of a landmark legal case that removes things like user interest and IP addresses from the category of protected health information.

WHY WOULD THESE PEOPLE CHOOSE ME?

You want your advertising to get in front of your ideal patients, but you have to ask, why would they choose to become *your* patients? Be bold and brutally honest when answering. You can't effectively market yourself if you can't answer this question. It's your job as the business owner to be able to explain why patients choose you. What makes you a better choice, even if it's just for some people, over your competitors? Be specific. Don't let yourself off the hook with perfunctory or vague ideas.

"We offer a different kind of patient experience," you might say. Okay, that's a start. Why do your patients value that experience? What is different about it? Is it a good experience but not truly unique in your market? If so, push further until you can be specific.

That process might lead to a conclusion like, "Our patients tend to be older clientele from affluent situations who live in nearby gated communities. Or they are upwardly mobile business professionals. They like that we don't treat kids or rush their care, and they like that we treat them much like guests in a five-star hotel are served. Our competitors have nice office settings but their team isn't as experienced in customer service and they happily take insurance that attracts family dentistry patients who want fast and cheap dentistry."

This gives you a lot of information that you can use to inform your marketing decisions. Keep an eye out for items that don't align with this answer as you track, analyze, and act on the data.

Then ask yourself…

HOW WILL I TURN LEADS INTO REVENUE?

You and your marketing team will be working your butts off trying to get prospective patients to contact your office, and you'll be investing a sizable budget to grow your practice. Let's assume that the marketing is a flawless success. You're dominating your region and patients are contacting your office multiple times every hour. That's the goal, right?

No! The goal is to increase your revenue. Phone calls don't pay the bills—production dollars do. You have to get patients in the door and they have to say 'Yes!' to treatment.

Some of the most common pitfalls after a dental office receives phone calls and emails from their marketing include:

- No one answers the phone.

- No one checks email, or calls and follows up on leads.

- The person who answers the phone is untrained in sales and customer service.

- The person who checks the email does not call the prospective patient before replying to the email, or does not do so in a timely manner.

- The person who operates your phones does not make scheduling appointments their top priority.

- Your team is not clear on why people choose you or does not stay on-message when talking about your office.

- Your team only acts as order-takers from patients and does not lead the conversation by presenting other services that you offer.

- Your team does not see your office's financial success as tied to their financial success.

- You or your team are not friendly and warm when interacting with patients.

All of these problems and more can sabotage marketing results, preventing new patient leads from turning into new patient revenue. No amount of marketing in the world can solve this problem. What's worse is that these create an internal marketing problem that breaks the Sales and Marketing Loop.

ACTION ITEMS

____Identify the last couple of tactical decisions you made about your marketing, then ask yourself if you would have made the same decisions after considering who you are targeting, why they would choose you, and how you will turn the leads into revenue. If you would have done something different, make a note to consider a change in direction on those items after you finish reading this book.

____Make a list of characteristics of your best patients and look at your current strategy for marketing and advertising. Note whether or not the strategy is likely to reach other future patients like them repeatedly and with a message that will appeal to them.

____Ask yourself why your future ideal patient would choose to become a patient at your office rather than your competitors. If the answer is "Honestly, they really might not," consider what changes you may need to make in your office or strategy until that answer is different.

____Analyze your current lead intake and note the holes in your process that could be wasting marketing dollars because leads are not turning into revenue.

Chapter 5

The Sales and Marketing Loop

YOUR OFFICE NEEDS a Sales and Marketing Loop:

1. Your advertising generates visibility.

2. Your marketing makes you attractive.

3. Your prospective patient contacts your office.

4. Your team schedules the consult.

5. Your team executes well on the consult, understanding the goals of the patient.

6. Your team books a new patient exam.

7. You and your team work well together during the new patient exam and present a comprehensive treatment plan.

8. Your patient sees the need for the treatment, understanding how it relates to the goals they expressed during the consult. They say 'Yes!'

9. You and your team provide excellent service during the treatment process, reminding the patient why they chose you and that they are achieving their goals.

10. You and your team celebrate the patient's treatment and get approval to share their photos and success story in your marketing.

11. Your team asks the patient for a review online and if the patient knows anyone with similar goals and personality. You would love to meet them.

12. You stay in touch with the patient for recare but also for referral opportunities.

13. Your patient's photos, reviews, and referrals feed back into steps 1, 2, 3 and so-on, driving more prospective patients to respond to your advertising, act on your marketing, and make new patients more likely to say "yes" to treatment.

This loop, when well-executed with a consistent effort, doesn't just go around and around. It accelerates, gaining lasting momentum. It's not very fun getting through the early years of this process, where you're spending energy launching a new campaign and then, like a baby learning to walk, you see ups and less-than-graceful flops. And yes, it really does take years to fine-tune a fantastic Sales and Marketing Loop, but keep in mind, I'm not talking about a website or an ad campaign—I'm talking about your marketing, advertising, dental practice, staff members, you and your patient base, all contributing to greater success than you've ever seen before.

It's like positioning a magnifying glass to start a fire. You want a fire and realize you've got this tool available that can do the job very well, all you've got to do is use it. But in order to use it, you've got to do a few things. You've got to find something to light: some kindling. You've got to then realize, shoot, I'm standing in the shade of a tree that's blocking the sun, so you choose a different spot. You get your kindling all set, and hold out the magnifying glass. The bead of light you're looking for isn't there. You've got a bright circle about a foot from where you stacked up the kindling, so you reposition the magnifying glass. Now you have some well-lit kindling but no smoke much less flames. So of course, you move the magnifying glass up and down until the bright circle shrinks into a blindingly-bright dot.

The problem is that many doctors never step out from under the shade or realize that they have this magnifying glass in their pocket. In this analogy, they're looking around asking, "Hey, anybody got a match?" They think that hiring a marketing company is going to bring about this roaring inferno of a campfire but they just occasionally get that match stick from someone, and they strike it on a nearby rock. It flames up. Hooray! And then it burns out. "Well that sucked," they say, and then go back to asking for another match.

I'm not saying that these doctors are too dumb to light a fire. They just don't even realize the insanity of the process—or rather they feel the insanity alright, and they want it to stop. They just want someone to light the freakin' fire so they can quit wasting time and go back to roasting marshmallows or whatever. Only you have the power to set yourself up for success by moving out into the sun, collecting more than kindling, some logs, building a windbreak, etc.

Figure out what you're cooking, and then go to town manipulating that magnifying glass. Marketing can help your office along the way, but you have to offer excellent dental services and train your team to contribute to (rather than detract from) the Sales and Marketing Loop.

A misstep along the way can break the loop. Too often, when new patient flow gets stopped up, the doctor looks at the marketing team for answers without scrutinizing the processes at their office. This is the equivalent of striking the match but watching it burn out without nurturing the tiny flame. Doctors who have the proper marketing mix and are using sound tactical decision-making in their marketing can tell that the leads are coming in. If you're saying to yourself, "Well, yeah, I'm getting leads but they're not turning into new patients," then first look downstream from the marketing.

Are you trying to light a rock on fire? Go through the Sales and Marketing Loop at the start of this chapter and look for a disconnect. You may find that there are actually many disconnects. You can't afford to fix just one or two. If you really want to win—if you really want to be happy coming to the office every day, you owe it to yourself and your team to fix it all.

Fixing these things can be painful and expensive, but it's critical to keep pushing for a seamless Sales and Marketing Loop in your dental practice. If you don't, it'll be even more painful and expensive as you spend money on ads that generate new patient leads doomed to fizzle. You'll treat the odd patient here and there and get an injection of production dollars that evaporate before they can multiply in referrals and marketing opportunities.

Pro Tip for Lead Intake: You cannot afford to generate leads that your team does not diligently pursue for scheduling appointments. Prospective patients have lives beyond their dental needs. This is especially true for elective dentistry. When someone calls your office, that's a fantastic, no-brainer opportunity to schedule a new patient appointment or at least a consult. But email leads and appointments scheduled online are tougher.

I have some offices who say that email leads are their best leads. Other offices say that none of their email leads ever pan out. What is the difference? How can both be true? The answer is in how the leads are handled.

When a prospective patient contacts your practice online rather than calling you, they are telling you two things: One: I'm interested. Two: I'm not quite sure what the next step is or when I can take it.

Focus on that first thing. The patient is interested, and know that it's your job to help them with the second, unspoken concern. Your team needs to call that prospective patient immediately and then touch base with the prospective patient multiple times in the following days. If you don't, you'll miss out on new patient opportunities. Call and email multiple times.

Scott Hansen, founder and CEO of LeadSigma, a new patient lead intake and follow-up platform, says that this kind of "multi-channel" lead follow up increases scheduled appointments from leads by 33%. He also says when an office calls the prospective patient right away (within 30 seconds), the chance of booking an appointment with that patient also goes up by about 33%. You can't just fire off an email that says, "Call our office if you're interested in scheduling an appointment." Doing so wastes marketing dollars and costs your practice revenue.

This is also true about appointments scheduled online. Treat them the same way that you would an email lead. Do not assume that they will just show up on the day of their appointment. Call them right away. Thank them for booking and confirm some key information. Doing so will decrease your no-show rate for new patient appointments. Your team will also be able to address situations where the patient may not be a fit for your practice, keeping your schedule clear for actual new patients. All of this adds up to more profit from your marketing.

Effective lead intake is critical if you want The Marketing Mix That Works to work for you.

WHAT IF I'M NOT A NATURAL-BORN SALES PERSON?

Most doctors went into dentistry because of a clinical interest or scientific mind. Maybe they were decent communicators too, but none of them went into dentistry because of their amazing sales skills. I know some dentists who discovered that they are actually pretty good at selling dentistry but they are few and far between. You are not alone if you're thinking, "I couldn't sell a hundred-dollar bill for a buck!"

You can hire your office's star sales person. A good practice management consultant can help you through this process better than I can cover in this book but having a good sales person is your secret weapon in marketing. Make sure that they understand what makes you great at what you do and teach them all they need to know about dentistry.

Proper training is critical to make sure that they don't shoot themselves (or you) in the foot. It will be a process to help them understand what is in-bounds and out-of-bounds for sealing the deal, but a natural-born sales person will quickly identify issues that will blow up a sale after the fact because they over-promised, potentially getting fired from a lucrative sales gig.

Your sales person does have to be incentivized by production dollars. They should make more than anyone else on your team, and your team should be incentivized by production too. Money motivates.

If you just put them on a base salary or ask your salaried assistant who also answers the phones and handles billing to also present treatment, you'll break the Sales and Marketing Loop. They won't be aggressive in presenting treatment, will look for the easy wins like single-tooth or quadrant dentistry at-best, and will not sell big cases.

Instead, hire a dedicated treatment coordinator who is incentivized to sell the type of treatment that you want to be known for. Bonus them for hitting specific goals and they will achieve those goals...or they'll leave on their own accord because they don't have the sales skills that you need. That can happen, but if you have all the systems in place and a handsome compensation and benefits package, you should have a good pool of people to choose from. They should even be eager to have the office's phone ring to their personal line after hours and on weekends because they know that they can boost their numbers by fielding as many opportunities as they can.

They will eagerly pursue these opportunities and close them as long as you don't sabotage their efforts.

YOUR SALES PERSON CAN'T DO IT ALL

You and your entire team need to be part of the effort to close the Sales and Marketing Loop. Just as your sales person needs to have the natural aptitude for sales, the rest of your team needs to have a natural aptitude for customer service. Balance clinical training with customer service and leadership training. If your team is just putting on scrubs, clocking in and out every day, without any vision for where they are going in life, they are unlikely to see how their work at your office is helping them to achieve their goals. They won't have any reason to go the extra mile. Extra miles—especially those that the patient notices—are what accelerate the Sales and Marketing Loop.

Have you ever read a stellar Google review? Here's a fictionalized review based on a real review that one of our clients received. Look for the "extra miles."

I feel refreshed after being at the dentist. How weird is that?! June at Dr. Smith's office is the best dental assistant I have ever met! She and Dr. Smith have exceeded my expectations in every way. My experience was better than any dental visit I have ever had. I am new to their office and was in pain but they calmed me down and changed the way that I will think of the dentist for the rest of my life. See you again soon, June, Berty, and Dr. Smith!

This person is a fan for life. The review will boost Dr. Smith's Google rankings and make people who check him out more likely to contact him. The review will also be great fuel for their social media efforts, and you better believe that when June presents a more comprehensive treatment to help the patient avoid future pain and to improve their smile, the patient will say "Yes!" The patient will also be more likely to agree to full-face photography to help the office showcase their amazing work.

All of this is thanks to the extra mile that June, Berty, and Dr. Smith went in how they interacted with the patient. I know the real "Dr. Smith" and I know that he has invested thousands—probably over a hundred thousand dollars in advanced training for himself and his team. They help him succeed and they know that they are a part of a dental office that is different than others in the area. They are also incentivized to deliver top-tier customer service, ensuring that patients will amplify his message in his market.

Pro Tip for Online Reputation Management: As you're seeing patients, listen for feedback and personally ask for reviews. Many patient communication platforms automate asking for reviews. When you turn that on, there's a temptation to think, "Well, that's handled. Now I can stop worrying about that." Don't do it. You'll get more reviews, and better reviews if you continue to personally ask for them. Simply explain how reviews help you reach new patients who don't know about your office and ask if they would be willing to do a review for you. Wait for a 'yes' so that the patient has to really think about whether or not they will do it and when. If you see some hesitation, press into the apparent conflict. Maybe their experience had an element in it that makes them hesitant to say good things about you. Take the opportunity to address it and turn the patient into a fan for life.

YOUR RELATIONSHIP WITH PATIENTS MATTERS

The patient looks up to you, doctor. Or at the very least, they put a lot of trust in you, especially when you are presenting and executing complicated, high-dollar treatment plans. You need to be likable and show personal interest in the patient. Work with your team to discover areas of common ground with the patient.

Keep that going with the patient when they leave your office. Have your team follow up with the patient to find out how they are doing. Send a thank-you note following treatment.

Stay in touch with them via email with newsletters that share what's going on in the office and useful information that may help tee-up future treatment presentation or prompt them to forward your message to a friend or loved one.

Build a relationship with them via social media. Appoint a social media leader at the practice who will send friend requests to patients after they meet them and who will engage with patients who comment on your social media posts. This leader should also have a goal set for taking pictures of you and the team at the office so that your social media builds relationship with your patients.

Without a great relationship, they are less likely to post that amazing review or refer the friend or family member who becomes your next big case.

Pro Tip for Social Media: Social media is only social if it has faces in it, and your patients love to see you in action. Show how your office can be fun and decidedly not-scary. This can happen with regularity if you add it to your processes. Do whatever it takes to make sure that social media, including Google Business Profile, gets updated with photos from your office on a regular basis.

YOUR MARKETING ADDS UP, AND HELPS GENERATE EXISTING PATIENT REVENUE

Imagine driving down the street and seeing a sign for a new restaurant. It appears to be your favorite type of cuisine. The next time you decide to grab dinner out, you decide to try the new restaurant. It's great. The food, atmosphere, and service are all wonderful. The following week, you drive by, and their sign is gone. Would you decide to call them to find out if they were still in business? The next time you wanted food of that type, would you just go there, even if there was no sign suggesting that the restaurant was still in operation? Maybe you would ask a friend about it, but if they had never seen the sign or experienced dining there, they would probably just shrug. They would have no idea.

At the same time, in this thought experiment, consider that you are passing by other restaurants with signs that represent restaurants you are familiar with as well, some that you like very much. There are also other new restaurants popping up with their own new signs. How long would it be until you stopped thinking about that spectacular dining experience and why their sign had disappeared? Eventually, you'd get hungry enough to go back to your restaurant faves or try something else new.

Your marketing works the same way that the restaurant's signage worked in our thought experiment. That's why businesses have signs—it's part of their marketing. But if you forget about, or even discredit, the value marketing brings in the form of brand awareness among your existing patient base, you're making a grave mistake.

Your marketing needs to generate new patients, but your marketing and advertisements impact existing patients to great effect. People are creatures of habit and won't casually hop from one dentist to another without a reason, but the reason doesn't have to be very big. If your Sales and Marketing Loop is broken, it can be as simple as a friend raving about one of your competitors and showing off some new veneers. If your patient hasn't seen you in a while, hasn't heard from you in a while, and then checks out your website only to find that it is unchanged since they first found you, it's easy for them to consider a switch.

Don't think existing patients check out your website? Don't think they interact with your ads? You need only check out your call tracking to discover that this isn't the case. Existing patients use your website all the time to find your phone number. They may even search the same keywords on the same platform that they used to find you in the first place, especially if they can't quite remember the name of your practice or doctor. If that happens, does the marketing get "credit" for that existing patient scheduling an appointment? Some marketing agencies believe so strongly that the answer is 'yes' that they will purposely target your practice's name with paid search ads. This is called branded search. They want you to be everywhere when someone searches your name, afraid that someone else's ad will come up and steal your business.

Your marketing builds brand awareness among new *and* existing patients, and this is a very good thing. This also means that, if you are doing very little marketing, your patient retention, recare, and production from your existing patient base are all suffering in addition to a lack of new patients. Do everything you can to get The Marketing Mix That Works in place and keep it in place as long as you are in business. If you don't, that's another giant waste of money.

Pro Tip for Sales Success: Start with why. Read Simon Sinek's book, *Start With Why*. It's a great read and a fantastic listen if you're into audiobooks. Read it and then reexamine your office's mission statement—or develop a separate Why Statement. Then start of every team meeting, including daily huddles, by going over the Why Statement. This should clarify why you are doing what you are doing the way you are doing it. Repeat exposure to this idea is critical. Change up the way that you share these concepts for maximum team retention. Quiz the team on the Why Statement, and have small rewards at the ready when they accurately recite the Why Statement. This vision for your business will help you when you develop your marketing as well, so be sure to share it with your marketing team. It should permeate your Sales and Marketing Loop.

ACTION ITEMS

___Consider each step of the Sales and Marketing Loop at your office. At each step, make a list of changes that you need to make. Because it is a loop, there is no wrong place to start, but look for improvements that carry multiple benefits.

___Take inventory of your team to identify your social media leader in your team and carve out time for them in your weekly schedule so that they can actually do this new facet of their job.

___Review your new patient paperwork and add a photo release form so that you will have written authorization to use their photos in your marketing, including social media.

___Hire a sales person to be your treatment coordinator. Work with them and a consultant as necessary until they can sell treatment to patients effectively and create a new workflow in your office to give them an opportunity to speak with patients. This is especially critical for busy doctors who do not have a sales bone in their body.

___Do not neglect making improvements inside the office to improve patient experience. Improve the look, smell, and even sound inside the office. Here again, a consultant can be invaluable.

CHAPTER 6

HOW MONEY CAN BREAK THE LOOP

AS I SAID IN THE INTRODUCTION, The Marketing Mix That Works will generally cost a dentist between $3,000-$6,000 per month. In hyper-competitive markets, to really break in, it will likely cost even more than that. You might be thinking, "I'm not spending a fraction of that. You're killing me!" I get that.

Money is important. You need a healthy business and deserve to take home every dollar of profit that you can. To achieve both of those goals, the integrity and acceleration of the Sales and Marketing Loop require money. The Marketing Mix That Works can still fail if it's underfunded.

With the Sales and Marketing Loop fully up to speed, marketing and advertising becomes so predictable, it runs like a math equation. You plug in the number of patients you'd like to see and the equation tells you how much money you should invest. For the sake of argument though, let's rearrange the equation and set the "How much should I spend?" variable to $0. Let's say that you eliminate advertising from the Sales and Marketing Loop. Deciding not to adver-tise means that you are at the mercy of the currents of Google and word of mouth marketing.

If you are content to keep your patient volume where it is, you might be able to get by if there are no other holes in your Sales and Marketing Loop. Without external marketing, internal marketing becomes even more crucial. Your patients are walking advertisements, eager to share the parts of the wins in their lives, so make sure that your practice wows them from the very beginning.

Even with your external marketing and advertising budget set to $0, money can break the Sales and Marketing Loop. As we said in the last chapter, you also need to invest dollars in a fantastic team that feels valued and sees the potential to do great things in their career with you. If you don't, you'll be stuck training new people all the time and the quality of your service will go down. Forget about extra miles—you'll be lucky if you're not broken down on the side of the road.

That's obviously not good enough, and you're not reading this book because you want to keep patient volume at the status quo. You're probably in a market that's at least semi-competitive. Even if you live in a somewhat rural area, you end up competing with larger practices in neighboring metro areas. You want to grow. Growth in your business requires investment.

Without regular investment, your marketing becomes ineffective. Websites stagnate. They require content updates and the occasional design refresh. Social media requires a lot of ongoing work. Even if you're taking a DIY approach to your marketing, *you* cost money. It's a lie to say that you work for free. If you do, I'd like to hire you.

Some doctors see money as a finite resource. They take an "it is what it is" attitude with their budget and are content to hope for the best, doing the same thing year after year, wishing things would magically change for them. I hope that's not you. If it is, I want you to take some time to consider what would make your life more fulfilling, or even help you sell your practice and move on from dentistry if that's where you are. Whatever it is, it will take investment, so you have to change how you think about money. Money is infinite when you are willing to change things.

RAISE YOUR PRICES

You can and should raise your prices. If your prices are dictated by insurance companies, consider renegotiating to a different plan with higher rates or dropping insurances altogether. We have several customers who operate fee-for-service dental practices. They will tell you that it wasn't an easy decision to go out-of-network with insurances, nor was it an overnight process, but they wouldn't have it any other way.

If your answer to the "Why do patients choose me instead of my competitors?" question before was, "Because I'm cheaper than all of my competitors," this presents a problem, but I hope that wasn't the case. If you are delivering the best *anything* in your area, your product shouldn't be the cheapest.

I don't care if it's a hot dog. If you sell the best hot dog in the city, your hot dog shouldn't also be the *cheapest* hot dog in the city! If you don't charge a premium for your premium service, it's only a matter of time before the quality slips and you're no longer the best.

I speak from experience. At Pro Impressions Marketing, we were charging a membership fee for our all-inclusive service that made us the most expensive dental marketing company dentists were considering in most cases. Not everyone hired us because of this but that was okay.

Then COVID-19 hit and we changed our business model to accommodate offices with smaller budgets. We started having to move to a volume model and our focus on quality drifted. In the wake of those changes, we lost some customers. The quality that we lost was not in our marketing services but in the customer service.

The type of office that said "Yes" to us also changed. Instead of bringing on fewer customers who paid for top-dollar, all-inclusive service with a concierge approach to client services, we had people come to us who said they "just needed a website." Remember, The Marketing Mix That Works is not just a website. They needed more and we had to accommodate, having to upsell them and worry about the profitability of building a low-budget website after having made change after change to the design.

We made the decision that, if we wanted to reach our goals and continue to be the best marketing company in dentistry, we had to back track and increase our prices, dropping the low-budget packages and services.

You may be saying, "But doesn't that mean you saw fewer new clients? If I raise my prices, I'll have fewer patients saying 'yes' to treatment." You're right, and there will be a period of adjustment as the Sales and Marketing Loop closes and gets up to speed. Your advertising and marketing should present a dental experience that appeals to your target patient with an emphasis on one or two services that you are passionate about. Then charge a premium for those best-in-class services that allows you to deliver those services in a premium capacity.

As you make that transition, start adding incentives and increasing salaries with your team. Because fewer patients schedule initially, you won't need as large a team. Maybe you'll want to keep it that way, but over time, word will get out. The Sales and Marketing Loop will accelerate. Patients will love you and tell the world about how you wowed them. Your return on investment from your marketing will improve with patients who invested much more than they would have before you raised your prices for the same services and they'll thank you for it.

Again, I know. We raised our prices and went back to a comprehensive marketing package. My team is going the extra mile and the customers are happier than ever. I don't mean that as a shameless plug. I just need you to understand that I know what I'm talking about.

I've seen dental offices do this and it works. It starts with you having another heart-to-heart with the dentist in the mirror and saying, "Gosh darn it, I'm worth it!"

If you can do this while contracted with insurances, that's fine. There is an upside to this as well. If you can negotiate better rates, find carriers who pay better, or get inventive with your processes so you achieve more revenue through more patients seen or treatment presented, you're still earning more revenue. You'll have an easier time converting leads into patients if you're in network. Just make sure that you make the changes necessary to fund meaningful growth and transformation in the practice.

FIRE ROBERTA

Your business supports you, your patients, and your entire staff's livelihood. You can't afford to jeopardize all of that by retaining a team member who is hurting your Sales and Marketing Loop.

One long-time customer has had a team member with him for literally decades. She is not a sales dynamo. She's an administrative workhorse—maybe even a work-a-holic. I have never asked the doctor point-blank, but I think he's also scared of her. We'll call her Roberta.

I'm certainly scared of Roberta. She's rarely in a good mood. When I call and she answers the phone, I inwardly groan. She never seems to have time for me, even when the doctor is expecting my call.

What's worse, when you listen to the office's calls, you can tell that the patients feel the same way. And, because she's all about the admin angle of things, she handles every call like a piece of paperwork rather than a sales conversation. She's about answering questions and getting back to what she's doing. Because of this approach, patients don't get booked for new patient appointments. They're turned off and happy to go back to their search and call someone else.

I told the doctor about this. I was elated when he hired a new office manager who started answering the phones. Something amazing happened: new patients were suddenly scheduling at a much higher rate than before! It was fantastic.

Then, inexplicably, Roberta started answering the phone again. I couldn't believe it. I thought that Roberta was history since she had been the office manager before—but no! The doctor had retained Roberta. Can you imagine the morale at an office where someone like Roberta had been effectively demoted. It probably wasn't much of a team at all.

And do you think that the doctor cut Roberta's salary? Of course not. The office was paying for two office manager salaries and Roberta landed back on the phones. The new patient appointment rate went back down, and the overhead at the office was higher than before, leading to even lower profit margins.

If you have an irascible team member who doesn't have a sales or customer service bone in their body; who doesn't seem to get along with the other team members; who may be mentioned by name in negative reviews even more than you, and who you're maybe a little afraid of—you *must* fire that Roberta.

Even if the chaos that ensues is hellacious, you'll be glad that you did and you'll improve the Sales and Marketing Loop in your office. If Roberta has "been there from the beginning," and you've been giving this staff member regular pay increases despite the problems that they've caused, you'll clear a bunch of payroll. This isn't why you're firing Roberta, but it is another symptom of an unhealthy part of your practice. You can use this increase in cashflow to hire that sales dynamo and maybe have some left over to put toward an advertising budget, feeding that dynamo more sales opportunities. Your team's morale will go up, and Roberta will probably be happier at her new job where things aren't changing. Robertas tend to hate change.

INCREASE YOUR MARKETING BUDGET

Easy for the marketing guy to say, right? Dental practices are different from many other types of businesses but they don't have the luxury of marketing themselves in a separate marketplace. They have to compete for the attention of consumers who are bombarded by marketing messages from non-dental brands as well other dentists, not to mention corporate and franchise dental brands.

Most dentists need to progress in their mindset toward marketing, if they want to see growth in their practices and if they want to mold their offices into a specific niche in dentistry. In an article by HubSpot that analyzed 2022 marketing trends, they looked at a survey by Deloitte and reported, "…if you work for a [product-focused] company, Deloitte reports 15.9% of overall budget is the average given to marketing teams — for [service-focused] companies, this is closer to 12%."

As an operator of a service-based business, if you have a $1,000,000 dental practice, 12% is $120,000. Maybe you can't swing that right now. Maybe sticker shock has blown the hair right off your head. But think about this: how much better might your practice's new patient flow be if you were investing closer to that? Do you think that the largest, most successful practices in your area are spending less than that? If they're running broadcast and cable TV ads, it's probably more.

The same HubSpot piece said of the Deloitte survey results, "If you work in the healthcare industry, you might expect to see a marketing budget around 7% of total budget." $70,000 is more than a lot of dental offices are spending, but it should be closer to the norm when you consider that the average cost of a new patient lead in healthcare can be as high as $287 or more. That's according to another paper from HubSpot and other myriad sources online.

At that average of $287, spending $70,000 over the course of the year, you would net only around 20 new patient leads per month. Of course, depending on how readily your team books appointments from your leads and the production dollars you get from new patients, you could be doing quite well for yourself at that level of investment. Still, why settle for the national average? The marketing mix that works includes data analysis for a reason. You and your marketing team should be able to buck the average unless you're in a hyper-competitive market and are leveraging the most expensive advertising tactics. Using The Marketing Mix That Works, Pro Impressions Marketing has achieved an average cost per lead of less than $100 for many practices we've worked with.

Assuming you have a sales dynamo and are charging well for your services, increasing your spending on marketing and advertising could do amazing things for your practice. You and your accountant just have to move from a finite mindset about money to an infinite mindset. Where is the rule that says you can't spend more than 12%? If it's netting you a handsome return, keep boosting the spend until you see a plateau.

Do the math for your own marketing budget. What percentage of your gross revenue is your marketing and advertising budget? If you don't know how much you're spending, start there. Pull together invoices. Be sure to ask about spend on ad clicks and media buys. What's the total? If it's 7% of your gross revenues or above, then you're probably doing okay, but also ask what it breaks down to for new patient lead numbers, case presentation and acceptance, and total production dollars realized.

If all of the numbers end up being underwhelming, you are probably breaking the Sales and Marketing Loop by underspending on the promotion of your office. It's a good place to start.

A dentist I know had a general and cosmetic practice that he was sick of running. That probably came through in his work and relationships with team and patients. I don't know for sure. I just know that it ended in bankruptcy.

He pivoted, launching a new practice focused exclusively on orthodontic treatment. It was a small office in a large city, offering very niche services. It would have been tempting, coming out of bankruptcy, to pinch every penny—maybe not even launch a website. He had to have been scared. Would history repeat itself? His cosmetic practice had failed. The temptation was there to either retire or go work for someone else just to collect a paycheck, but he saw that he had a second chance.

He didn't pinch pennies. He launched a new, high-quality design with new content. He jumped in with SEO and social media marketing. He even launched online ads and paid up to retain the team of the office he bought to invest in loyalty and experience.

The investment paid off. Google loved it. People loved it. The office continues to thrive today because he continued to invest in marketing, and as the office has continued to grow, he has invested more in paid search and social media. Because his Sales and Marketing Loop is really moving, his cost per lead is less than 20% of that national average, at about $23 per lead over the last 60 days at the time of this writing.

INVEST IN PAID VISIBILITY ONLINE

Budgets for Google Ads, or sponsored visibility in social media, are some of the most overlooked investment opportunities in all of advertising. I railed against them years ago as an internet marketing consultant. They used to suck. Flat out, they were expensive and they didn't seem to work well.

That was nearly two decades ago. A lot has changed. Google has refined its advertising platform with scary-good algorithms. Almost every other online search service has too, including many that provide strong alternatives to Google such as generative AI search platforms.

When you start talking about something and see an ad for it, you may hate how Big Brother is watching, but for many, that's just the norm. And as creepy as it may be, you can bring that magic to bear for your office when you have the right people in charge of your campaign *and* you hand those people enough money to actually leverage the services to their full potential.

If you've tested the waters with these types of services, perhaps years ago when Google Ads was Google AdWords, and you saw poor results. Like I said, it sucked back then. It could also be that the ad specialist you hired did a poor job with targeting—*double suck!* It could also be that when you tested the waters, you didn't give it enough budget.

Google will spend any budget you give them. When properly targeted, their platform may complain that there aren't enough clicks to spend the full budget, but in general, for dental keywords, there's enough Google search traffic to spend thousands of dollars—often tens of thousands of dollars. If there's an opportunity for Google to earn that kind of money, the top positions in their ad results will likely go to advertisers willing to invest at those levels.

What about the little guys? The ones who only want to spend a few hundred dollars a month? Google will take their money too. That's why they include the ad positions at the bottom of the search results and ads at the top of page 8. They get clicked on, but not generally by people who are serious about finding a dentist anytime soon.

After you've found a marketing team that you trust, feed your online visibility with serious ad budgets. This will help ensure that you close the Sales and Marketing Loop. You'll get more visibility and you'll get *more frequent* visibility. More people will see your ads again and again. That repeat exposure will blow up your website with tons of traffic.

If you're worried that this type of exposure will net you the "wrong type of patient," stay in touch with your marketing team about your results. Also train your team on how to identify the real ask from potential patients. Sometimes people who call for teeth whitening are really interested in the dazzling smile that can only be achieved with restorative dentistry. They just need an education and they need to know that you care enough to give them the time of day.

On social media platforms like Meta's Instagram and Facebook, ad budgets are less likely to generate new patient inquiries unless you have a low-dollar offer of some sort. Still, ads can ensure your posts are actually seen and that you're achieving the maximum brand-building potential of social media. Without that repeat exposure, on social media or elsewhere, you'll find your website traffic suffers and your phones are quiet. Unless your office is already well-known in your city, unpaid visibility usually doesn't pay the bills these days.

Pro Tip for Google Ads: Remember to avoid marketing ADHD. While Google Ads is a pay-to-play platform, there are a lot of similarities to Google's organic algorithm. Campaigns take a while to build up steam.

When a new campaign is launched, Google places it in "learning mode." That's Google's name for the period when their algorithms are figuring things out. Campaigns tend to under-perform in "learning mode," but there's no way to skip it. And, when you make a change to a campaign, it goes back into "learning mode." So, if your ad management team is constantly making changes, the campaign will never go anywhere. Be sure to give Google Ads at least three months after you launch them before you make sweeping changes, and then another three months to analyze the impact of those changes. By sweeping changes, I am referring to the launch of a new campaign, a shift in keyword targeting, a change in budget, or a shift in geographic targeting.

Give Google's algorithm time to *assess* what you've asked it to do, time to *actually do* what you've asked it to do, and time to *evaluate* its work and *adapt* to the results. Only then can you do the data reporting and analysis of the actual outcome of the changes you've made. If you let marketing ADHD influence your decision-making, you'll end up nipping your own success in the bud before it comes to fruition. You must be patient, even with Google Ads.

INSURANCE CAN MAKE OR BREAK THE SALES AND MARKETING LOOP

Your team must also be trained to answer the most common question from new patient callers, "Do you accept XYZ Insurance?" Regardless of whether or not you are in-network with any specific insurance, your team needs to understand that, in the U.S. anyway, people can see any dentist they wish, regardless of their insurance. Your team already knows people believe their insurance is much more generous than the insurance company actually is—so why let them go on being ignorant?

You can see a patient with an HMO or Medicaid without participating in those networks or programs, right? The patient will have to pay out of pocket, of course. They may choose to spend their money on something else instead of your treatment, sure. That is the patient's choice—not the insurance company's, not yours to make for them, and not Roberta's choice either. The *patient* has the right to choose, and they should be able to make that decision with all the information available to them.

Would you rather your best friend be seen at an office like yours or the cheapest office in town that takes Medicaid? There's a difference between your office and most of those offices, isn't there? Isn't the difference worth the extra expense? Your best friend deserves the opportunity to choose, and so do the people who call your office.

Not everyone will choose to become your patient, and not everyone will have the funds for a new patient appointment when they call.

But people will find the money for the dentistry that you present if they see the value you offer and feel they are valued as a potential patient. You will slow down the momentum of your office's Sales and Marketing Loop if you and your team prejudge callers because their first question is, "Do you take XYZ Insurance?"

At Pro Impressions Marketing, we listen to our office's calls to categorize them into Existing Patient Caller, New Patient Caller, Wrong Number calls, etc. So, we hear how our customers handle their phone intake. Sometimes, it's super cringy.

"Thanks for calling Illustra Care Dental. This is Laura. How can I help you?"

Hi. Do you take PrimeraCare Insurance?

"No, I'm sorry."

Okay. Thank you. [CLICK]

Listening to one of those calls, I want to slomo-scream, "Nooo!" I want to rewind time, pause it, and tell Laura: This new patient caller may have all the funds in the world. They may be looking for an office just like your dental office, and they may be absolutely fine filing a claim with their insurance company on their own and taking what they can get. They might be interested in coughing up 80 grand in cash for full-arch, multi-implant dentistry…and you just let them off the hook!

Instead, that call should go something like…

"Thanks for calling Illustra Care Dental. This is Laura. How can I help you?"

Hi. Do you take PrimeraCare Insurance?

"I'd be happy to check into your insurance benefits for you. Who do I have the pleasure of speaking with today?"

Shelby.

"Thank you, Shelby. And what prompted you to call us today?"

From that moment on, the call isn't primarily about money. It's about the patient and their needs, and it's a call that Laura is steering rather than the patient. Laura just needs to know that she isn't an insurance coverage bot. She's a treatment counselor, if you will, helping the people in her area get the best treatment they possibly can for their dental needs—ideally making Illustra Care Dental their new dental home.

Of course, it's possible that Shelby—notice that in the first scenario, Laura didn't even learn Shelby's name—is broke as a joke and expects to get free dental implants. But Shelby might not *always* be broke, and Shelby needs to know that spending money on dental implants is a better investment than the next great iPhone or VR headset.

Handling the phones is an entire book topic, so I won't go into all of the scenarios I hear where patients are turned away, discriminated against, turned off, or pissed off because of assumptions made by the team member who takes the call, but it's a common problem. The bottom line is that *assumptions kill production dollars.* Insurance just happens to be the biggest assumption that patients and dental teams make.

Now, if you *are* contracted with dental insurances, you are obviously setting up your dental business in a different way than a fee-for-service office. You'll need to see patients in a higher volume to make up for some thinner profit margins, but the good news is that this insurance bugaboo that so many offices struggle with is much less of an issue. You can simply say, "yes!" and move on to getting Shelby's name, but I highly recommend that whether you are in-network or not, you redirect the conversation to be about the patient's needs and how you can help them.

Eventually, you have to address whether or not you are in-network with their particular insurance program. My favorite response to this is, "We have many patients with XYZ Insurance. What we do is..." and then lay out the patient's journey in your office, ending with how the patient gets top-notch care and has their dental problem solved. Keep the main thing the main thing, and the main thing you want the conversation to be about is dental care. Whether the patient becomes a patient at your office or not should be based on need and values—not whether or not *the insurance company* says they can get care at your office.

ACTION ITEMS

___Look into when you last raised your prices and consider raising them to make financial room for the decisions you need to make that will shore up the Sales and Marketing Loop in your office.

___Fire your "Roberta" if you have one. This will lift morale at your office, boost new patient appointments, and free up payroll for your next rockstar employee. Be brave enough to get through this conflict, knowing that better times are on the other side of this.

___Calculate your current average cost per lead with your existing marketing and advertising spend. Establish this number as a month-by-month average for the last 12 months. A lead is a phone call, email, or online appointment request. Tally up your marketing and advertising investment for the month, then divide it by the total number of leads your office received. This number is your average cost per lead.

Be sure to eliminate things like wrong number calls, existing patient calls, spam emails, etc. Do not eliminate things like new patients who called but did not book, or people who did not show up for their appointments. While those are frustrating, you will not be able to adapt marketing to avoid those, so trying to cook the numbers into only tracking home-run outcomes will only skew your numbers and lead to bad marketing decisions. Finally, compare your average cost per lead to the national average of $287 and look for any trends you can find in those averages. Talk with your marketing team about your findings to try to improve things.

___Take inventory of what you really want to achieve with your practice from a personal standpoint. Dream big and write it down. Then consider, "How much money would I spend to buy that dream?" If you can come up with a number, write that number down under that dream, and consider how much less you've been investing in your marketing. Increase your marketing investment so that it's more in-line with your dreams.

____Invest time in listening to your calls and training the team who takes new patient calls on how they answer the "Do you take XYZ Insurance?" question. Be sure your team breaks the habit of pre-judging prospective patients. If you don't feel capable of training and role-playing phone issues with your team, invest in a consultant or other team training that will accomplish this for you.

Chapter 7

Dental Marketing and Sales Forecast

WHEN I SPEAK WITH DENTISTS about their marketing and the possibility of becoming a Pro Impressions Marketing customer, they often ask, "So, if we move our marketing over to you, what can we expect? Like, how many more new patients will we get?" This question is almost impossible to answer, but I like where their head is at.

We've talked about the marketing and sales loop and how that can impact your marketing results. We've talked about the patient's experience with the office and the doctor. We've talked about how money can feed or starve your marketing and advertising. Hypothetically, let's say that you got an A+ in every category. What will the result be?

Exact numbers are still impossible to give to even an individual dentist, but you can establish a forecast. Just like it's important to track your results, it's a good thing to try to forecast what your sales will be. Setting such a goal means that you know what's in it for you, and you're more likely to be enthusiastic about the prospects.

Set aside actual numbers for a minute. We want to build a sort of algorithm that will help us establish the likely trajectory of dental demand in your area and how that will funnel down into new patient revenue at your office. When you have this algorithm, you can plug in some rough numbers from estimates and traffic to see what sort of opportunity is there and then make decisions on how you can improve the outcomes.

Start with national trends. The marketing mix that works taps into demand. Traditional media can create some demand for your services when you launch it at scale, but the most economical approach is to tap into the flow of people who are seeking out dentists. The easiest place to track that demand is online.

Every market is different, but since it can be difficult to peek inside the collective mind of your local community, understanding dental demand at large can give you a feeling for how people in your area are perhaps leaning. It's not definitive data, but it's based on real, human input.

Go to trends.google.com. Or you can go to google.com and search for Google Trends. This tool, provided by Google, allows you to "Explore what the world is searching," according to their website. Google Trends doesn't give you exact numbers of how many people searched for any given phrase, but gives you numbers that show a relationship between the number of people searching for a term or phrase at different time periods.

For example, the tool shows a search volume of 2 for the topic of

Ukraine in January 2014, and a relative search volume of 100 for Ukraine in January 2022. Monthly interest has generally bounced around between 6 and 10 ever since. So, there was a giant, nearly 100% increase in search interest in Ukraine when Russia invaded. We don't know exactly how many people are included in the 100-level search volume number, but we know it's a lot.

Now, put in 'dentist' in the search bar and click on dentist as a search term. Google allows you to alternatively look at how many people are interested in dentist as an occupation, but that's not helpful for our purposes. We want to know how many people are performing dentist-related searches. This is still very broad, but we are looking for trends. We can narrow this focus, but to start, let's look at broad trends.

By default, when you perform a search on Google Trends, it shows Worldwide data for the past 12 months. This is a start, but now we want to narrow things to try to get more useful information. Click on the 'Worldwide' dropdown under 'dentist' and change the Region criteria to your country. I'll assume you selected 'United States.' Now that you have data for the United States, click on the date range drop down. Select '2004 to present.' Look at that beautiful upward trend. That's why you bought this book. The opportunity in digital dental marketing just keeps growing.

You'll also notice, along this upward trajectory, large peaks and valleys. These happen for a variety of reasons. Many of the peaks are seasonal. The January search volumes are almost always much higher than the preceding months and then trend downward until July. July search volumes typically peak up after the 4th of July.

If you hover over July in 2015, you'll see that there was a large peak. That jump in searches corresponds with the news about Dr. Walter Palmer's fateful hunting trip to Africa when he killed Cecil the lion. Lots of people started Googling things like 'dentist who killed a lion'. Similarly, April is normally not a time when dentist-related searches go up, but in April 2022, a dentist was charged with his wife's murder on a hunting trip in Africa. Search volumes for his name plus 'dentist' went up over 600%, skewing the data again. We saw the same thing happen in the summer of 2025 when he was convicted of the murder and sentenced to life.

Set the time range to 'Past 12 Months' and notice the vampire-fang shaped teeth in the graph. These show how traffic bottoms out around the Thanksgiving and Christmas holidays in the USA. This doesn't necessarily mean that your marketing will have no results during those time periods, but if you look at your website's traffic during those times, you probably see a decline as well.

Now click the large '+ Compare' box and type in the word 'cars,' then select 'Cars - search term.' This shows that the search volume for the topic of cars is much higher than searches for dentist. This comparison data isn't very actionable but illustrates how Google Trends can be used to compare the search volumes for different search terms and phrases.

Click on 'cars' at the top of the page and change it to dental implants and select the 'search term' option again. You'll see that many more people search for 'dentist' than 'dental implants.' Makes sense, right? Now, change 'dentist' to 'porcelain veneers' as a search term. 'dental implants' crushes 'porcelain veneers.'

Scroll down the page and you'll see some maps that highlight the relative search volumes in a state-by-state breakdown for dental implants and porcelain veneers. Notice that, in the Interest by Subregion section for porcelain veneers, some of the states are grey.

Google Trends explains this on their website:

INTEREST BY SUBREGION

See in which location your term was most popular during the specified time frame. Values are calculated on a scale from 0 to 100, where 100 is the location with the most popularity as a fraction of total searches in that location, a value of 50 indicates a location which is half as popular. A value of 0 indicates a location where there was not enough data for this term.

This is why looking at national trends is helpful and sometimes our only option when it comes to looking for trends Local data is sometimes unavailable or just so sporadic and low in numbers that Google Trends can't really give us useful information.

Sticking to national trends, you can continue to compare search trends and see that 'dental implants' is a juicy target while 'porcelain veneers' and 'cosmetic dentistry' may be search phrases that are more top of mind for dentists than they are for the average joe or jane. This can help you make strategic decisions and forecast potential increases in your results over time.

In larger states, you can check state-level data to see if the national trend is echoed closer to home. Some states are so unique that this isn't feasible. Alaska, while a geographic giant has an economy all its own that doesn't always match up with the rest of the country. Hawaii is also more challenging to track, but so is Vermont, so it really doesn't have anything to do with being within the contiguous states.

Now let's look at 'Invisalign,' Align Technology's banner trademark that has become a household name for clear braces everywhere. After you've selected the search term, set the time range to '2004-Present' again.

When times are turbulent, forecasting dental interests is a challenge. You're better off looking for repeated trends in historical data to try to make sound decisions and set realistic goals.

Looking at the data, we can see that online interest in Invisalign has continued to climb. If you change your time range to Custom and set it to the last two years, you'll probably see some seasonal trends.

Let's pretend that we are making a marketing and sales forecast for your dental practice and it's September. You want to know how the rest of the year is likely to shake out and you're considering a new ad campaign to boost Invisalign numbers. These national trends tell us that:

- While the late summer, back-to-school interest in Invisalign is usually nice, it's unlikely to continue that increase into the last quarter of the year.

- October will probably be a ho-hum month.

- November could show a little promise but that the Thanksgiving holiday will ding us a bit. We should also consider how election hype could impact us as political ads flood the market.

- The last week of the year might not be too bad if we have

someone in the office to field calls and schedule patients for appointments after the New Year.

Aside from the holidays, there's some opportunity here.

Once you know whether or not people are likely to search more frequently for the upcoming quarter based on the previous period on a national level, you can track that back to your website and overall campaign.

Ask yourself:

- How much traffic has my website been getting so far on a monthly basis this year? Average out the best months with the worst months.

- How many leads am I getting from the current efforts on an average monthly basis?

- Am I doing everything I need to in order to turn those leads into patients?

If all of those answers are good, and you are considering an increased investment in marketing and advertising, as long as the trends forecast a good seasonal outlook, you have reason to be hopeful for an increase in new patient numbers.

In this hypothetical Invisalign scenario, however, if you decided not to invest more in the new Invisalign marketing campaign and instead just left your marketing the way it was, I would not forecast an increase despite some potential peaks there. The summer often shows elevated interest compared to October through December, and the two holiday periods could potentially eat away at those peaks. Without an increase in ad visibility, there's not much reason to expect a higher forecast for new patients. In fact, it might be more realistic to forecast steady new patient flow with an increased spend and a decline in new patient flow without the added visibility.

The longer the timeline on a campaign, the more likely I would be to forecast success because you are able to course-correct as you go and adapt to the changes in your market, not to mention repeat exposure with prospective patients who have seen the ads but not yet converted.

Factor in real-world issues at your office and be honest with yourself about their impact on the Sales and Marketing Loop. For example, look at new patient appointment bookings when you, the dentist, are out of the office. If they are down because you have no one at the office when you are away, then you have to temper your expectations if your forecast includes a time when you will be out of the office.

If you are working with some new team members, know that they might need some ramp-up time to get good at lead intake. You may be able to adjust your plans for training and team scheduling accordingly to mitigate these in-office impacts, or you could choose to pull back your marketing investment during those periods. Before you do, consider this: the dentists we worked with who kept their marketing going during the 2020 pandemic office closures tended to have their best years ever in 2021 compared to offices who did not market during those times. As in our restaurant thought experiment, these dentists had their signs flashing while others had theirs essen-tially taken down.

Going back to the algorithm, keep it as simple as possible. Set a time period like we were doing in Google Trends. We need to identify how many months we want to measure. Let's use a quarter (3 months). Now how much of an increase in demand are you seeing in that forecast? Be conservative, yet optimistic where you can. If you always assume a negative outcome, you'll never launch any marketing, and we know that this is a recipe for achieving the status quo—if you're lucky. Let's say we think there's a 20% increase in demand for the time period.

If our marketing taps into that demand increase, and we're already achieving 10 new patients per month, is it reasonable to expect that we can achieve a 20% increase from 10 new patients? Yes, I think that's very reasonable. So, 12 new patients, instead of 10. We're not setting the world on fire at that level, but it's progress.

If you're doing zero advertising and you tap into the market with a well-executed advertising strategy, careful to give it time to mature, by the end of the quarter, you'd likely see a much larger increase than 20%. That's because your visibility didn't just increase by 20%. Your visibility went from 0% to 100%, and that's something to get very excited about.

At a 20% increase in new patients over three months, how much more revenue would your office achieve? And consider that, because of the Sales and Marketing Loop, if your office executes well on those new patient visits, each one of those patients becomes an ambassador of your practice, helping your marketing perform even better with new photos, reviews, and referrals.

Your visibility also has long-term impact on your brand awareness because of repeat exposure. Every time a potential customer is exposed to your brand via an ad, a map listing, or social media post, it becomes more likely they will take action to contact you (a conversion). This means each piece of marketing your brand puts out (an impression), becomes even more valuable. It's easy to lose sight of this when you forecast short time periods and make overly conservative tactical decisions.

Instead, use forecast information to identify potential for bolstering campaigns rather than trying to avoid spending on painful periods. You can instead prop up those lulls with ad dollars and really capitalize on times when the fish are biting by spending more time at the lake with more lines in the water.

I'm not saying that the answer is always to spend, spend, spend. Forecasting new patient leads and sales is all about setting your expectations so that the tracking of outcomes is more meaningful. To stick with the fishing metaphor, you could always bait your hook, toss in the anchor, wet your line, and take a nap. If you do, don't be surprised if, at best, you wake up with only one fish on the line, or more likely, your bait is gone and you pull up a bare hook. Instead, set a more attractive lure and keep casting until you hit your daily limit. If you do, you'll be more likely to come back the next day.

Pro Tip for Online Advertising: Be wary of advertising companies that use landing pages and funnel tracking software as the basis for their advertising platforms. There is nothing inherently wrong with these tactics, but the companies that employ them tend to focus less on true patient leads. They view every person in your "funnel" in their program as a new patient, whether you speak with them or not— often without even having a phone number you could use to call the patient. Instead, these companies often present a lot of other numbers like impressions or subscribers as indicators that the campaign is doing well. They love to take a brute force approach to the campaigns and say, "You have to be patient."

In my experience, ad results are better on your main website than with landing pages (also called squeeze pages). People want to be able to see your team, your office, your reviews, and your before and after photos. They have certain expectations of what a dental office website feels like, and these landing pages often feel more like they're selling a widget or asking you to download a whitepaper.

If the user experience is different, the user will behave differently. We always have to remember the intent behind people on the internet. Your ads *should* target people whose intent is to find a provider, and your website should be built to convert those people. Ads that target people in an info-gathering stage, where they have a looky-loo intent, will not convert well to butts in the chair.

Add to this the technical headaches of having launched what amounts to another website, and this becomes an easy no. Who needs another website to update with new photography, or to worry about potentially throwing Google's indexing for a loop if it's not coded correctly? We've seen that happen, and it can get very messy. Google can mistakenly assume that you're doing a website redesign and your current website can suffer in Google visibility as a result.

Perhaps the best reason to be leery of a company with their own funnel system of ads > to landing page > to lead management system, is that it interferes with lead tracking. In The Marketing Mix That Works, you track leads in one central location. If a company is running ads external to that system, you'll have leads in two or three places. This sets you up for failure.

ACTION ITEMS

___Try out Google Trends at Trends.Google.com

___Identify a new campaign that you are considering, or set a hypothetical marketing campaign goal in your mind, and try to forecast what you could expect in your practice if you were to launch a marketing campaign targeting a specific group of phrases.

___Consider the revenue that your office generates from a new patient in the category you want to target (general dentistry, dental implants, etc.), and consider how an increase in those patients could impact your office's financial situation. How much would you invest in marketing to achieve that change?

___Identify real-world issues in your practice such as time out of the office or new hires and recent team departures (bye Roberta!) that could impact your marketing while your practice adjusts to the change.

CHAPTER 8

"HOW MUCH SHOULD I SPEND ON MARKETING?"

I'VE HEARD DOCTORS SAY, "I would be happy if I could just get X number of patients per month." This is a great thought. It's part of an equation that you should use in calculating your spend. It's similar to what Stephen Covey said about beginning with the end in mind or more recently, what Drew Hinrichs and Barbara Stackhouse, in *Profit First for Dentists*, wrote about paying yourself your profits before paying any other bills.

Figure out what you want in new patients and work your way backward. As we talked about in Chapter 2, you must identify your target patient. That's important but financially speaking, what's the goal? This may seem overly simplified, but do some rough math with this equation below to identify "Z money," or your profit goal.

$$X \text{ target patients } (Y \text{ your fee} - E \text{ expenses}) = Z \text{ money}$$

Your profit is your goal. Again, read *Profit First for Dentists* for more on this, but you need zee money to be happy, no? Start with Z money. What will make you thrilled to come to work every day and help you to afford the lifestyle that you want? Figure out how much money you want to bring home in a year, or during a given period such as a six-month campaign designed to bolster patient numbers in a specific area of your practice. Then work backward.

How many will you need to bring in to achieve your profitability goal? You just need to do the math. What's your overhead for each patient, and how many patients will you have to get to exceed your overhead and achieve your target profit? You don't have to do your accountant's job. I'm not suggesting that you become a bookkeeper as well as a marketing expert. This equation is merely designed to help you set some goals while also giving you a target figure for lead numbers. This number will ultimately help you answer the "how much should I spend?" question.

Here's an example. My fictitious dental practice is called Illustra Care. I'm going to set my *Z money* goal as $150,000, meaning that I want to add $150,000 in profit in the coming year on top of what I'm already achieving in the practice. To achieve this, Illustra Care is launching a new marketing campaign that seeks to add more general dentistry patients to the practice who also need restorative work. Our goal for fees charged will be $250 for a new patient exam, including x-rays, and $2,800 for restorative work. Some patients will say yes to more treatment. Some will just want a hygiene appointment. That's okay.

Z money = $150,000

Fees = $3,050

I am going to do a rough calculation of fixed overhead per patient by dividing my current monthly payroll, utilities, insurance, and anything else that is a set expense that doesn't really fluctuate month to month based on the number of patients that Illustra Care sees in a given month.

$$\text{E expenses} = \frac{(\text{Rent} + \text{Utilities} + \text{Payroll} + \text{Insurance} + \text{Other Fixed Costs})}{\text{Total Unique Patients Seen}}$$

If you're a savvy business owner, you may notice that I didn't include marketing in that equation. Marketing isn't free, of course, but your marketing expense will vary depending on how many patients we end up targeting, so we'll account for that by identifying the available marketing budget and dividing the available marketing budget by the number of new patient's we want to attract. If that cost of patient acquisition seems unreasonable, we'll know we have a problem on our hands.

For now, Illustra Care's expenses look like this:

- Rent: $75,000 annually

- Utilities: $6,000 annually

- Existing Staff Salaries/Benefits: $420,000 annually

- Insurance: $4,000 annually

- Other Fixed Costs: $105,000 annually

I'm also seeing about 2,500 patients annually. This means that, calculating my expenses looks like this:

$$\$244 = \frac{(\$75,000 + \$6,000 + \$420,000 + \$4,000 + \$105,000)}{2,500}$$

E expenses per patient = $244

Remember, the equation we are trying to solve is:

X target patients (Y fee - E expenses) = Z money

So, our updated equation looks like:

X target patients ($3,050 - $244) = $150,000

$$54 = \frac{\$150,000}{\$2,806}$$

X target patients = 54

Remember, I'm planning on some of these patients having restorative work, so let's also factor in lab fees. I'll assume a crown or two and a bill of $300 from the lab. Maybe that's much higher or lower than what you get from your lab. That's okay. You'll do your own calculations using your numbers.

Here are Illustra Care's updated numbers:

X target patients ($3,050 - ($244 + $300) = $150,000

$$59 = \frac{\$150,000}{\$2,506}$$

X target patients = 59

The more my expenses are, the more patients I have to see to achieve my goal. So, of course, the higher my fees are, the fewer patients I have to see. But if your fees are astronomical, you have to be honest with yourself on what your conversion rate will be in-office. Consider nudging down your fees and know that you'll have to make up the difference with a little more volume, or figure out where you can trim some fat, especially if the overhead corresponds with serving non-target patients that you hate.

Now where will you put these patients? Don't skip steps like scheduling for these patients. The details could break the Sales and Marketing Loop if you're not careful. Keep working through the journey that patients take as they see you until you get to how they heard about you. Now you're ready to actually calculate marketing and advertising costs.

Start by calculating your budget. Does your budget change how much marketing costs? No, but it will determine what type of marketing campaign you can realistically launch. Marketing is only frustrating when the campaign doesn't meet the needs and expectations of the dentist who launched the campaign. We're going to set a budget for Illustra Care that we will use to attract the 59 new patients that I need in order to achieve my goal.

Maximum Marketing Budget = [X Target Patients (Y Your Fee- (E expenses Per Patient + L Lab Cost Per Patient))] - Z Money

$-\$2,146 = [59 (\$3,050 - (\$244 + \$300))] - \$150,000$

-$2,146? Well, crap! That's not going to work.

This is the problem that so many dentists and marketing people don't solve—or at least, they don't solve it together. If you can't balance this equation without turning things upside down on one side or another, then the campaign won't work!

Let's see what happens when we reduce our profitability goal. This can be necessary if your profitability goal is unrealistic given the state of the market or given the state of the practice. Your profitability should never be zero or negative, but if you're staring down a negative number and you feel like your overhead is a trimmed down as it's going to get anytime soon, you often have no option but to settle for a lower figure for Z money, at least for a time.

$$\$87,854 = [59\ (\$3,050 - (\$244 + \$300))] - \$60,000$$

This says that I can achieve $60,000 in profit if I can bring in 59 new patients at $1,474 each ($87,854 max budget ÷59 new patients) and if I can get at least $3,050 in treatment from them while keeping my overhead under $544 per patient. That might be mission impossible for your practice. That's okay. Work the math, knowing that you only need to be accurate enough for your marketing plan to make sense. Find what would work for you, then work with your marketing company to find a way to achieve this repeatably. Your accountant can help, but they don't tend to see marketing as anything but an expense. Instead, you're putting on your entrepreneur hat and using money to make money.

Remember, you need to get out of the fixing a sink or betting on a horse mentality. You're making a marketing plan that is built you're your business processes. Make an ongoing investment in marketing and advertising that keeps your visibility up, thus keeping target patients flowing. In the end, the equation you wind up with will depend on these factors:

- The state of your marketing now and whether or not it needs an overhaul.

- The competition in your area for the target patients, including the cost of ads by keyword in digital ads, especially paid search ads on Google.

- The volume of target patients you want to generate and the number of visits or ad views and clicks you need to generate before one of these target patients contacts you.

- The number of these new patient inquiries that you need to generate in order to get a patient on your schedule. This goes back to the Sales and Marketing Loop and having dynamos on your team to schedule the right people and get them to say yes.

Also remember that these calculations aren't a one-and-done event. You'll need to keep track of this as part of your Data Tracking and Reporting, but again, don't feel like you need to do it alone. Involve your marketing team. Even in the sales process if you're considering a new company, they should be able to give you a range to work with.

For our dentists, I've told them that a realistic marketing investment ranges from $0 up to $30,000 per month just for Google Ads, but that all comes down to the location of the office and the keywords that they want to target to bring in their desired, target patient. If you're considering a marketing company that specializes in doctors like you, they should be able to narrow the range once you give them some details, but reputable companies may only be able to tell you what they charge, then give you a budget estimate. Once you get up and running, through data tracking and analysis, they'll be able to tell you if the budget is sufficient or if it's not enough to stay competitive and achieve the numbers that you want to achieve.

Now, let's add the marketing costs to our calculations. Expanding the simple equation above, the 'How much?' math becomes:

$$(X \text{ patients} \times \$Y \text{ fee}) - (\$C \text{ ad budget} + \$M \text{ marketing} + E \text{ expenses})$$
$$= Z \text{ money}$$

The more complex this becomes, the more you'll be tempted to involve your accountant in the plan, and that's okay. But don't let them take over and do this *for* you. They should work *with* you on it, and not against you. If your accountant has a hard time seeing money spent on marketing as anything but overhead, they may just want to reduce your marketing budget as much as possible.

Looking at the equation above, obviously, if an aggressive marketing and advertising budget outstrips the revenue on the left side of the equation, Z money will evaporate. I'm not a CPA. I'm a marketer and I can still see that's bad.

Still, everyone involved, the marketing team, the doctor, and the accountant all have to play a role in balancing this equation in favor of making your practice as profitable as possible.

- The marketer who is quarterbacking the ads and marketing must be accountable for keeping the new patient leads flowing.

- The doctor must be accountable for setting appropriate fees to stay profitable and for having a team that gets patients on the schedule and saying yes to treatment.

- The accountant has to support the doctor in identifying when it's time to raise fees and where they can trim costs that will make room for a marketing budget that will ultimately boost Z money.

In the ideal scenario, when the marketing and advertising really hum, occasionally, the marketer or even the accountant might broach the question about boosting the spend on ads to increase revenue and a savvy doctor will know that the answer has to hinge on the patient experience. If there is no room on the schedule, and patients are feeling effectively turned away because they can't be seen for months, or if the doctor and team are running wild between operatories, sterilization, and lab rooms, seeing so many patients at one time, the quality of the care will slip. The team will start to forget to take photos and ask for referrals and reviews. They may even struggle to answer the phone when it rings.

If it would damage the patient experience to increase patient volume, the answer has to be "no" because it could break the Sales and Marketing Loop and then actually negatively impact Z money rather than boosting it.

WHEN YOUR PPC BUDGET SHOULD = $0

Since you're in Chapter 8 of a book about increasing new patients, you're probably not worried about attracting *too many* new patients. You might be drowning in the wrong type of patient. Or you might be getting leads and not able to get a single patient to say 'yes' to treatment.

Unethical advertising professionals who are just in it for the quick buck won't like this, but if you have problems that are preventing you from generating revenue from new patient leads, then set your ad budget to $0.

That's right. The author of a marketing book and owner of a marketing company just gave you permission to *spend zero dollars on advertising*. An ad budget that doesn't generate new patient appointments is a giant waste of money.

Keep your website up and running, but stop work on all other ongoing marketing while you fix the problems in your practice. Fix them fast or you'll go broke from your other overhead because your new patient revenue will continue to also be close to $0. The problems that are causing leads to die on the vine before they can be picked are strangling the future of your practice.

Start by firing Roberta, and look closely at your schedule to be sure that you're leaving room for new patient appointments until it's absolutely necessary to fill them with existing patients in need of single-tooth dentistry. You may also need to spin up some training for the team and enlist the help of a consultant to bring about the change that you want in your practice. You are the leader in your office. You set the tone. Let the team know that it is not business as usual anymore: you're in it to win it, and good things are happening.

Pro Tip: Traditional Media in The Marketing Mix That Works When you can add traditional media to The Marketing Mix That Works, it's a thrill. Because successful marketing is about repeat exposure, traditional media can help you add more exposure in your market, acting as an offline bridge between online encounters with your brand. Television, radio, and even billboards can also be amazing demand-generating tools.

However, I started the previous paragraph with 'when' because traditional media is usually an expensive proposition, and if you don't have The Marketing Mix That Works in place, and you haven't shored up your Sales and Marketing Loop, investing in traditional media can be wasteful. You'll see inefficiencies that—well, you won't actually see the inefficiencies unless you're using the tracking in The Marketing Mix That Works—but they'll leave you speechless. You'll have spent thousands of dollars on ad buys and be told that your ad was seen by thousands of people, but you won't have the patients to show for it if you don't have the proper marketing mix that works in place and have a Sales and Marketing Loop that is already beginning to sing.

On the other hand, I've worked with offices that have been running traditional media for years and are used to the inefficiencies I'm talking about. They're oblivious to just how bad it is. When we've implemented better online marketing and pointed out the holes in their Sales and Marketing Loop, the sudden increase in leads can be incredible—sometimes overwhelming. This sudden increase comes because we've plugged the holes that are causing the inefficiencies and the traditional media is doing what it was designed to do all along.

If I had my way, every practice that I work with would give traditional media a try for six months or so, and would do it right. Scraping the bottom of the barrel with ad buys at odd times of day or on irrelevant channels is a waste of marketing dollars. It's much like online advertising in this way. You have to fund the budget appropriately, and you have to make sure that the frequency of plays of your commercial is high enough to register for the average viewer or listener. When you do this, and you are patient and let the repeat exposure build, you'll see your lead numbers across all of your marketing mediums—even patient referrals—go up.

ACTION ITEMS

___Identify your current average quarterly revenue per patient seen for the past four quarters. This looks like total revenue for 3 months divided by the total number of patients seen during the same period. Do this for January–March, April–June, July–September, and October–December of the past twelve months.

___Use the same process to find your average cost per patient using fixed expenses: monthly expenses that never change regardless of how many patients you see. Include average lab costs if your average patient has at least some lab cost.

___Identify how many new patients per month you are achieving on average.

___Identify a goal for profitability for the next 12 months.

___Using your average new patient numbers, per-patient expenses, and revenue per patient, when you subtract your profitability goal, identify your maximum marketing budget.

___If you don't know it already, identify what your current marketing spend is so that you can see what your marketing cost per patient is and how much higher or lower your current marketing is when compared to your maximum marketing budget.

___Work the equation above to create goals for a new marketing campaign that targets an increase in new patients, fee, and profitability, as well as a decrease in expenses.

___List additional action steps that you identify as necessary to achieve those changes and to launch this new marketing campaign.

CHAPTER 9

YOUR NEXT STEPS

WE TALKED ABOUT THE MARKETING MIX THAT WORKS. You have that recipe. But now, where do you start?

FIRST THINGS FIRST

Even though you and others follow this same list of recommendations and steps, your path to better marketing success will be unique to you. That's why trying to mimic other doctors in their marketing approach doesn't work out for most offices.

Your first step should be to tackle the Sales and Marketing Loop. Marketing a practice with problems downstream from the marketing is unsustainable and wasteful. So, work backwards. Look for places after the marketing where sales break down. That might be getting patients to agree to treatment. It might be the in-office experience.

Whatever it is, you have to get your practice to a place most people—maybe not all, but most—will love.

If money is standing in the way, you have to figure out some way to get that flywheel started. I'm not a business coach, so I can't say the best way to do that, but I understand the conundrum. Quality talent and nice office furnishings cost money but without a steady flow of profitable patients, it's hard to make that money. It has to come from somewhere.

The danger in putting all of your money into marketing is that, without the team and quality in-office experience, it will likely only come with an infusion of busy work. Your leads will fizzle before they turn into revenue. So, start small with whatever you can, work your way up, and never stop. Fire Roberta, turn your marketing budget to $0, and use the money from both of those things to make the other changes you need, whether that's the office décor or team training.

Turn your existing patients into super-fans who will refer you more business. Continue to wow them and then raise your prices until you have more margin to work with as a marketing and ad budget.

IF YOU HAVE YOUR OFFICE WELL-IN-ORDER

Congratulations. This is the time to start knocking out the other challenges that are holding up new patient flow. Tackle the Challenges You Know About in Chapter 2 from top to bottom. Don't skip around. For your convenience, here they are again:

1. Beware a lack of strategy and communication with your marketing team.

2. Avoid brand disconnects.

3. Don't update your marketing without a plan.

4. Don't be blind to competition.

If you don't remember what that means, invest more time in Chapter 2. As you re-read, take notes on what challenges you have that are staring you in the face. With this book, you should be able to pick them apart more easily.

Then start looking for self-sabotage holding back your practice. Again, for your convenience, those Chapter 3 items are:

5. Avoid "Marketing ADHD." Until you've got everything else nailed down, don't make another change in your marketing unless your current company is incapable of helping you get things fixed.

6. Be aware of vicinity issues. "Location! Location! Location!" is a real issue even in digital dental advertising. You cannot afford to ignore it.

7. Does your reputation precede (and screw) you?

8. Do you look like a dentist to Google?

9. Are you buying into the hype (and accidental lies) of a colleague who is bragging about their amazing marketing? Don't do it. Do your own investigative work as to whether or not the new shiny strategy will work for you. While you want to avoid marketing ADHD, dropping something that doesn't fit because of the above issues is still prudent. It will free up budget to spend on marketing fundamentals.

These lists will likely take you some time to work through. That's okay as long as you are making progress. Some things may be outside of your power to change. That's okay too, but then you'll have to figure out how to offset that issue's impact. For example, if your office's vicinity is a problem, you may have to spend more to expand your reach or find other creative ways to attract patients from the other side of town. If your local patients aren't enough to keep your pipeline full, and patients are driving or flying just to become your patient then...

YOU'RE NO LONGER WASTING MONEY ON MARKETING!

Again, congratulations. You have joined an elite class of doctors. You can be confident that all you need is input for now—more new patient leads. You need to really get that Sales and Marketing Loop churning. Use The Marketing Mix That Works. Those marketing pieces are:

1. Search Engine Optimization (SEO)

2. Online listing management so that your online profiles are complete and leveraged properly.

3. Online reputation management, including a review cultivation strategy of some sort.

4. Google Ads (formerly called Google AdWords), a paid search advertising platform. Do the "How much" math from Chapter 8 to determine a budget.

5. Social media marketing that combines your office's own activity with management of a social media agency that can extend and multiply your efforts.

6. A data tracking process that includes regular account-ability meetings between you, your office manager, and your marketing company.

This all assumes that you have a great website. You will have addressed that while refining your marketing plan and branding. If somehow that wasn't something you tackled yet, then consider that...

YOU MAY NEED A NEW WEBSITE

Websites are like fishing lures. They come in all shapes and sizes with different types of attractive features and hooks. Most important is that it's something that your marketing company (including the advertising company if you have a different person running your ads than the company who manages your website) can work with. You should like your website, but even if it's not your favorite, if your marketing and advertising people think it works and can get you results, in the end that's what really matters.

Your website needs to align with your brand which stems from your clear strategy. The patient and Google need to understand who you are and what you do. There are also some key features that every great website shares:

- Clear, prominent, and consistent branding throughout every page that makes it *your* website.

- Easy-to-use navigation/menu buttons that have zero-learning curve. The average senior citizen should be able to use your website.

- A phone number and/or call buttons that are obvious and easy to access without a lot of extra clicking or scrolling.

- Original content that showcases what makes you great at what you do. The amount of text will vary by subject but know that, at the time of this writing, you still need a decent amount of text on each subject you'd like to target if you want to get organic rankings on Google.

Beyond that, your marketing and advertising companies are the boss. I won't tell you that it must be built in a certain platform or have a certain number or arrangement of pages. Different dental marketing companies are successful using different website construction strategies. As long as you use the full marketing mix and don't skip the data tracking and accountability meetings, you'll know if the website needs to be changed from a technical or management standpoint.

You also need to understand that your website is part of a larger marketing and advertising strategy which is part of the greater Sales and Marketing Loop and...

It's all a Work in Progress, Always

You are shoring up the Sales and Marketing Loop. It has to be done, and it's all okay. It's your job as a business owner and that will *always* be a work in progress. Your website is never done. Your SEO strategy is never done. Your ad strategy better not be static or you're wasting money. It's *all* a work in progress. You'll never be able to just set it and forget it if you really want to be successful and stay that way.

Imagine a beautiful water fountain. Water is pushed up from a source, jets to the top. Then gravity starts to win out and pulls the water back down to the source. What happens if you turn off the pump?

The Sales and Marketing Loop requires constant fuel and attention to keep it going. Systems will make that work efficient, as well as having the right people in place to work in the various roles, but nothing lasts forever. Gravity, entropy, life—*something* will start to win out and you'll have to continue to tackle those issues. That doesn't mean that you're not moving forward toward your goals.

Keep working at the challenges in front of you. Be vigilant about the things that once made your marketing a giant waste of money. You'll be okay. You'll be more than okay. You're going to dominate your area. Your patients will love you, and you and your team will love what you're doing.

Marketing FAQs

Why is this other dentist doing so well? What's he doing?

Neither you nor your marketing company can truly know why this other dentist seems to be doing so well, and trying to copy their marketing won't work. Instead, consider what makes this other dentist's office so apparently desirable. If these desirable aspects fall in line with your goals and practice's brand, you can copy that and make your office just as desirable, then make sure that these new aspects of your practice shine in your marketing.

How do I know I'm not just going to waste my money?

When you start by making changes in your practice to ensure new patient leads will be booked and turn into revenue, you take away the variable of whether or not your marketing and advertising strategy will generate leads that don't convert to revenue in your office. Then, when you create a marketing campaign that accurately markets your practice based on clear communication, the campaign is much more likely to generate patients who book new patient visits and say yes to treatment plans. All that leaves is avoiding self-sabotage. Chapters 2 and 3 are your friends.

WHY DOESN'T MARKETING JUST *WORK*?

I know, right? Patients are living in a chaotic world with countless demands on their attention and budgets like never before...and yet, marketing sort of *does* just work when you have proper expectations, use The Marketing Mix that Works, and give it time. The oldest principle of marketing is repeat exposure. If your marketing mix is tuned to the people your practice serves and you give those people time to see your message again and again, it will work.

And when I say 'proper expectations' that means that you have to have agreement with your marketing team on what "working" means. Sadly, many dentists have a false belief that marketing will fix a lot of problems that really are business problems—not marketing problems.

To ensure that that's not happening to you, have an open and honest conversation with your marketing team about why you signed up and what you want from your marketing. The marketers you work with should be able to tell you straight-up if it's all-systems-go and you just need to give it time, or if it's "mission: impossible," and it's time to revisit the relationship.

HOW CAN I GET A WEBSITE THAT DOESN'T HAVE TO BE REDONE EVERY OTHER YEAR?

Some website designs are more timeless than others, but even those are only going to last three or four years before they really start showing their age. The real reason though, that you're probably asking this question, is that you're finding yourself changing marketing companies every other year. That's not good.

But staying focused on the website aspect of the question, when you switch marketing companies, you are asking them to take over the entire marketing effort. In order to do their best work—and not have room for excuses if the results are underwhelming, they need to be able to work with a website that meets all of their needs. They're going to want to set things up just the way they want them.

WHY CAN'T I JUST USE MY CURRENT WEBSITE?

Think of it kind of like a new patient telling you that they are switching dentists and want to be your patient, but they want you to come and treat them at their old dentist's office using their equipment. That'd be ridiculous of course, but marketers feel the same way about this website problem. There's the layout of the office, the tools and equipment that aren't their preferred make and model, the tray set-ups aren't what they want, and they have no idea where supplies are or who the assistants are. Marketers have specific standards for platform, code, plugins, and other ways of making their work more effective and efficient.

Your marketing team should try to make this a low barrier to entry for you in terms of time and investment cost, being more focused on the long-term relationship than trying to gouge you for a giant website investment. Just know that, if the team is right, then any investment in setting them up for success from Day One is money and time well spent. That may just mean starting from scratch.

WHY IS MARKETING SO EXPENSIVE?

Much of the cost of marketing is set by…the market, and the market makes these services expensive because they really can generate amazing results. That drives up the demand for marketing but the supply of marketers is finite, and the costs of tools required to be successful go up over time as well. There are a lot of parallels between dentists and marketers as business owners, actually. You both fight overhead and the constant tug between the business of running a business and doing the actual work (i.e. clinical dental work) that got you into the business in the beginning.

But truly, especially where ads are concerned, demand for dentistry drives up competition which drives up costs. The good news is marketing done in line with the recommendations of this book will generate a multi-fold return. Marketing is only expensive when it's done with poor planning, is poorly executed, run without attention to the Sales and Marketing Loop, or some combination of all of those issues.

HOW MANY PATIENTS CAN I REALISTICALLY GET PER MONTH?

It depends. I'm sorry. I wish I could give you a definitive answer, but it's a function of the location of your practice, the treatment you want to do, the nature of your office, the scope of your campaign and budget, and the time of year. Still, you could create a very rough and very conservative estimate if you use the national average cost per lead in healthcare $250-$300. Using those numbers, you could calculate the number of patients (very expensive patients, granted) that you might be able to generate on a monthly basis by dividing your marketing and advertising budget by those numbers.

Hopefully your marketing team is more effective than this and your practice is not located in an ultra-competitive market. Those are variables that I just can't account for in this book except to say that Pro Impressions Marketing does regularly beat that national average, scoring new patient leads for our offices for less than $100.

WHAT IS THE BEST WAY TO ATTRACT NEW PATIENTS?

Use The Marketing Mix That Works. Respect the Sales and Marketing Loop—but only rely on these after properly preparing your office for marketing success. See Chapters 2 and 3 on those challenges that would thwart even the best-executed marketing and sales effort.

WHAT IS THE SECRET TO MAKING SOCIAL MEDIA SUCCESSFUL?

First, determine what success is. No, seriously. Ask yourself why you even want to run a social media campaign with your office. Write down the goals that you'd like to achieve and talk to your marketing team.

This fundamental question is critical because some dentists see being a social media influencer as the goal. To become an influencer, you need an entirely different plan for operating your profiles, different kinds of content, and different metrics for success that will be a giant waste of money for the average dental office.

I have to ask, "How many dental influencers does Instagram need anyway?"

What most dental offices need—the secret to social media success for the average dental office—is for the dentist to show up on their social media platforms with their face and to do so consistently as part of their weekly operations. It doesn't have to be expensive or a big-time investment. It just needs to be personal and consistent.

Get doctor in front of a camera doing their thing. If you, doctor, are very camera shy and don't want to talk, then just have your team video you as you work.

If you need help, just Google Pro Impressions Marketing and go to our social media page. But, um, if you're trying to become a dental influencer, don't Google Pro Impressions Marketing. Call our competitors instead.

HOW CAN I MAKE SURE MY SCHEDULE STAYS FULL WITH NEW AND RETURNING PATIENTS?

The recommendations in this book support both new and returning patient appointment generation. Depending on the type of practice you're running, the more common problem that I find lately is that offices don't leave room for new patient appointments. The most successful offices that I've worked with have always juggled their schedule so that they can fit a new patient in pronto. This ensures that you are seeing them when their interest in solving their dental problem is at its peak. If your team is trying to book them months out, then you'll likely schedule fewer new patients when they call.

Be sure to check out Chapters 2, 3, and 6 for common ways that dentists end up accidentally sabotaging their marketing efforts, leading to schedules with gaping holes.

WHAT IF MY MARKETING DECISIONS END UP HURTING MY PRACTICE INSTEAD OF HELPING IT?

This is a legitimate concern if your practice has other fundamental issues. As I mention in Chapter 8, sometimes, your budget for advertising should go to $0 while you focus on preparing your practice for marketing. When you've got the practice shored up, you'll notice that new patient numbers start improving even without marketing being in place. That's a good sign that your practice will be fruitful soil in which to sow some marketing dollars.

If you don't do that, you could very well launch a marketing campaign that is a giant waste of money, further taxing an already stressed dental practice (and dentist), and even making things worse because the patients you do see are leaving negative reviews. This will make the phones ring even less frequently than they already are.

WILL I EVER BE ABLE TO RETIRE IF I DON'T GET MY MARKETING RIGHT?

Okay, this isn't a question that I'm asked frequently—not in so many words. But I do talk to dentists all the time who are working much later into their careers than they anticipated. Marketing can very much inject new life into practices and prime them for sale so that you can hang up your handpiece and enjoy a payout at the end of a long career. If you don't market well—and run your business well—then you might be on the treadmill until you physically can't practice anymore.

Fortunately, I've only seen this happen once, and it was kind of by design. The dentist was happy practicing for a long time, and didn't want to keep the practice running at 100% capacity. Consequently, the practice didn't amount to much when it came to brokering it for sale. With no real takers, he ended up signing over the patient base to a dentist in town for a song, liquidated the equipment as best he could, and put the building up for sale. I don't know if the dentist has any real regrets, but I would have liked a bit of a bigger pay day if I were him.

To do it over again, if I were calling the shots, I would have had him put his nose to the grind stone for a couple of years at the end, build up the new patient flow with marketing—even signing with some insurance companies if need be—and getting things really humming on the balance sheet, and the practice would have sold more readily for a higher price.

HOW DO I KNOW IF INVESTING IN MARKETING WILL ACTUALLY BRING A RETURN ON MY INVESTMENT?

You'd really need to add a time period to the end of this sentence to know the answer. All marketing campaigns take time to mature. So, be honest with yourself, and your marketing company, by asking "When can I expect to start seeing a return on my investment?" Or "What can I expect in terms of ROI within the first 6 months?" The specificity will ensure a much more productive conversation.

But again, with time (give a from-scratch campaign a year), using The Marketing Mix That Works, and having a well-tended-to Sales and Marketing Loop, you have every reason to expect a return on investment. Our customers easily see a 6X return, and some see a better than 10X return, but they didn't see that in the first six months.

AM I ALREADY SPENDING TOO MUCH MONEY ON MARKETING? HOW CAN I TELL IF I NEED TO CUT BACK OR ADJUST MY BUDGET?

Take time to do the math. Any accountant should be of the mind that, 'spending too much on marketing' means that you're not seeing the production dollars tick up alongside the marketing spend. Calculate your total patients seen and total production dollars on a monthly basis for the last 2 years, and then drop in your monthly investment in marketing and advertising. Do you see an uptick in patients seen and production dollars following a change in marketing? If you cut marketing, did you see patients and production go down? If so, the marketing was doing something. How much did it decline or increase following the change? Look for patterns.

Do not bother trying to track every marketing dollar from the marketing medium directly through to new patient production dollars. If you do, you'll drive yourself crazy. It's never that clean and you'll wind up drawing erroneous conclusions.

One other thing about pay-per-click advertising that my team and I have come to understand: Google will happily accept everyone's money but unless you really come ready with a decent budget, you have every reason to believe that the campaign will be a giant waste of money—especially if it's only a few hundred dollars per month.

I wouldn't typically recommend running a Google Ads campaign for less than $1,500 per month in actual click budget, meaning that Google is able to charge your credit card for up to $1,500 every month. This seems to be the budget threshold in dentistry for most markets where the office is getting decent placement and frequency such that the clicks are converting into leads at a decent clip.

There's much more that goes into how we run campaigns than just telling the doctors, "You need to spend more." But if you're spending less than that, there's a decent chance that you should adjust your budget: either to $0 or to talk with your ad team about what they could do with a few thousand dollars per month. Just make sure that they can speak intelligently to how they will manage the extra budget.

What if I sign up with a marketing company, pay them a lot of money, and get nothing in return?

Nothing? It would be extremely rare to get nothing. But I have picked up the pieces from marketing companies that made grave mistakes in their customer's marketing and actually did send the campaign backwards in visibility and phone calls to the practice. The only way that you can avoid this is by getting to know the company very well. Ask for references. Understand what their plan is and make a generally well-informed decision rather than a knee-jerk decision to move to a new company based on a single pitch or special at a conference.

Still, "nothing in return" makes me think that the heart of the question is more about expectations. Have that conversation with the marketing team: what are you hoping to see in results and let them tell you whether or not they think you're being realistic.

What if I spend money on advertising, the phone starts ringing, but I still don't get new patients?

If that happens, you missed the step on communicating with your marketing team about who they are targeting and for what type of dentistry. You also need to examine your Sales and Marketing Loop. If your team isn't booking appointments, listen to the calls. Are patients being offered an appointment? "I have an opening on Tuesday morning if you'd like to come in?" is awfully hard to turn down. Find out why the patients aren't booking, then, unless it's a quick fix (i.e. our ai-powered phone tree was pissing people off and now we're going to answer personally), you might as well pause the ad campaign until you can solve the problem.

HOW DO I KNOW IF MY PAST MARKETING EFFORTS WERE A WASTE, AND HOW CAN I AVOID MAKING THE SAME MISTAKES?

Your past marketing efforts were probably not entirely giant wastes of money—only somewhat. No, seriously, they may not have been entirely efficient, but *some* visibility is still *something*. You just want to keep learning from your mistakes and improving. When you hire a new company, they will have never marketed a practice exactly like yours. Even if you hire Pro Impressions Marketing, they will probably never have worked with you. Your practice is slightly different than others, and your market adds another layer of variables. It will take anyone time to study your practice, then study the early data coming out of the campaign, and make the proper adjustments.

I will say that dental marketing specialists like Pro Impressions Marketing are going to be safer bets overall than general companies out there because they have had time to hone the art and the science of marketing dental offices over time. People are pretty much people wherever, so learning the market (your city) will have less of a learning curve than understanding that some keyword phrases are just never going to make a dentist money.

Phrases like "What shape were stegosaurus teeth?"! Seriously, some marketing companies have no concept of what drives patients to an office versus how to get someone on your website. Work with someone like that, and your advertising campaign will be a giant waste of money. Instead, use a company that really understands The Marketing Mix That Works.

CAN I HIRE YOU TO BE MY WEB GUY, JONATHAN?

No, not exactly, but I own an excellent dental marketing company called Pro Impressions Marketing. Check them out online at ProImpressionsMarketing.com.

ABOUT THE AUTHOR

JONATHAN FASHBAUGH is the author of many articles and books on a variety of subjects. He is the founder of Pro Impressions Marketing and the co-author of *The TMJ Trifecta: Solving Your Pain Puzzle*. He has written for Dental Economics, Dental Entrepreneur, The Ortho Tribune, Inside Dentistry, Dental Sleep Practice magazine, and many others. He is also a novelist, writing books about fascinating characters who go through funny, exciting, and sometimes tragic events while they learn more about who they are. Follow him on Amazon, Instagram, and TikTok to learn more about when he releases new content and to find his current works.

Jonathan lives in the Missouri Ozarks, in the town of Mansfield. He and his family enjoy worshipping Jesus and exploring His world through homesteading. They are avid board gamers and love to read. Jonathan and his wife, Amanda have been married for more than 20 years and have 8 sons.

You May Also Enjoy

The TMJ Trifecta: Solving Your Pain Puzzle

by Dr. McHenry "Mac" Lee and Jonathan Fashbaugh

Help Your Patients Solve the TMJ Puzzle

If you've ever had a patient present with chronic headaches, jaw pain, neck pain, ear problems, or facial soreness—and your exam revealed little more than "possible TMD"—you know how frustrating TMJ cases can be.

That's why I co-authored The TMJ Trifecta: Solving Your Pain Puzzle with renowned TMJ dentist, doctor Mac Lee. This book is written for patients, but it's also a tool for dentists and their teams. It helps patients understand:

- ✓ What TMJ disorder really is (and isn't)

- ✓ How jaw problems can create symptoms throughout the body

- ✓ Why so many treatments fail—and how to avoid common mistakes

- ✓ Practical self-care steps they can take right away

8. How to find the right kind of provider for lasting relief

Now retired, Dr. Lee treated thousands of TMJ patients in his

50+ years of practice, and the book distills that experience into a clear, hopeful roadmap for sufferers. You can hand it to a patient who feels stuck, use it to reinforce your treatment recommendations, or simply keep it on hand as an educational resource.

Get your copy on Amazon or in audiobook format. Just search "The TMJ Trifecta book," or use this QR code: